More Programming Pearls
Confessions of a Coder

More Programming Pearls
Confessions of a Coder

Jon Bentley

AT&T Bell Laboratories
Murray Hill, New Jersey

ADDISON-WESLEY PUBLISHING COMPANY

Reading, Massachusetts • Menlo Park, California • New York
Don Mills, Ontario • Wokingham, England • Amsterdam • Bonn
Sydney • Singapore • Tokyo • Madrid • San Juan

To Daniel Timothy Bentley

Library of Congress Cataloging-in-Publication Data

Bentley, Jon Louis.
  More programming pearls.

  Includes index.
  1. Electronic digital computers--Programming.
I. Title.
QA76.6.B452 1988   005   87-37447
ISBN 0-201-11889-0

Copyright © 1988 by Bell Telephone Laboratories, Incorporated.

This book was typeset in Times Roman and Courier by the author, using an Autologic APS-5 phototypesetter driven by a DEC VAX 8550 running the 9th Edition of the UNIX operating system.

DEC, PDP and VAX are trademarks of Digital Equipment Corporation. UNIX is a registered trademark of AT&T.

ABCDEFGHIJ-HA-898

PREFACE

Computer programming is fun. Sometimes programming is elegant science. It's also building and using new software tools. Programming is about people, too: What problem does my customer really want to solve? How can I make it easy for users to communicate with my program? Programming has led me to learn about topics ranging from organic chemistry to Napoleon's campaigns. This book describes all these aspects of programming, and many more.

This book is a collection of essays. Each one can be read in isolation, but there is a logical grouping to the complete set. Columns 1 through 4 describe techniques for manipulating programs. Columns 5 through 8 present some tricks of the programmer's trade; they are the least technical in the book. Columns 9 through 12 turn to the design of input and output. Columns 13 through 15 describe three useful subroutines. More details on these themes can be found in the introduction to each part.

Most of the columns are based upon my "Programming Pearls" columns in *Communications of the Association for Computing Machinery*. The publication history is described in the introductions to the various parts. Given that early versions already appeared in print, why did I bother writing this book? The columns have changed substantially since they first appeared. There have been literally thousands of little improvements: there are new problems and solutions, little bugs have been fixed, and I've incorporated comments from many readers. Some old sections have been removed to reduce overlap, many new sections have been added, and one of the columns is brand new.

The biggest reason for writing this book, though, is that I wanted to present the various columns as a cohesive whole; I wanted to display the string of pearls. My 1986 book *Programming Pearls* is a similar collection of thirteen columns, built around the central theme of performance, which played a prominent role in the first two years of the *CACM* column. The topic of efficiency rears its head in a few of these columns, but this book surveys a much larger piece of the programming landscape.

As you read the columns, don't go too fast. Read them well, one per sitting. Try the problems as they are posed — some of them aren't as easy as they look. The further reading at the end of some columns isn't intended as a scholarly reference list; I've recommended a few books that are an important part of my personal library.

I am happy to be able to acknowledge the substantial contributions of many people. Al Aho, Peter Denning, Brian Kernighan and Doug McIlroy made detailed comments on each column. I am also grateful for the helpful comments of Bill Cleveland, Mike Garey, Eric Grosse, Gerard Holzmann, Lynn Jelinski, David Johnson, Arno Penzias, Ravi Sethi, Bjarne Stroustrup, Howard Trickey, and Vic Vyssotsky. I appreciate receiving permission from several people to quote their letters, particularly Peter Denning, Bob Floyd, Frank Starmer, Vic Vyssotsky, and Bruce Weide. I am especially indebted to the ACM for encouraging publication of the columns in this form, and to the many *Communications* readers who made this expanded version necessary and possible by their comments on the original columns. Bell Labs, and especially the Computing Science Research Center, has provided a wonderfully supportive environment as I've written the columns. Thanks, all.

Murray Hill, New Jersey   J. B.

CONTENTS

More Programming Pearls

Confessions of a Coder

PART I: **PROGRAMMING TECHNIQUES**

I don't have the patience to save the best for last. These four columns deal with the best part of the programmer's job: those blissful hours you spend at the keyboard, staring at a computer screen.

Column 1 shows how profilers can provide insight into the dynamic behavior of programs. Column 2 is about associative arrays, a powerful data structure. Column 3 describes the scaffolding used for testing and debugging small subroutines. Column 4 presents methods for making data files self-describing.

These techniques deal with real programs, so they have to be illustrated in a real language on a real system. Column 1 uses the C language, and Columns 2 and 3 contain several Awk programs. All examples are in simple subsets of the languages. For readers who feel uncomfortable with the programs, Appendix 1 sketches both C and Awk. But even though the illustrations are in those languages, the techniques can be used on any system.

Column 1 appeared in the July 1987 *Communications of the ACM*. Columns 2 and 3 were published in June and July 1985, together with an early version of Appendices 1 and 2. Column 4 appeared in the June 1987 issue.

COLUMN 1: **PROFILERS**

The stethoscope is a simple tool that revolutionized the practice of medicine: it gave physicians an effective way to monitor the human body. A profiler can do the same thing for your programs.

What tools do you now use to study your programs? Sophisticated analysis systems are widely available, ranging from interactive debuggers to systems for program animation. But just as CAT scanners will never replace stethoscopes, complex software will never replace the simplest tool that we programmers have for monitoring our programs: a profiler that shows how often each part of a program is executed.

This column starts by using two kinds of profilers to speed up a tiny program (but keep in mind that the real purpose is to illustrate profilers). Subsequent sections sketch various uses of profilers, a profiler for a nonprocedural language, and techniques for building profilers.

1.1 Computing Primes

Program P1 is an ANSI Standard C program to print all primes less than 1000, in order (see Appendix 1 if you don't know C):

```
              int prime(int n)
              {    int i,
999                for (i = 2; i < n; i++)
78022                  if (n % i == 0)
831                        return 0;
168                return 1;
              }

              main()
              {    int i, n;
1                  n = 1000;
1                  for (i = 2; i <= n; i++)
999                    if (prime(i))
168                        printf("%d\n", i);
              }
```

The prime function returns 1 (true) if its integer argument *n* is prime and 0 otherwise; it tests all integers between 2 and *n*−1 to see whether they divide *n*. The main procedure uses that routine to examine the integers 2 through 1000, in order, and prints primes as they are found.

I wrote Program P1 as I would write any C program, and then compiled it with a profiling option. After the program executed, a single command generated the listing shown. (I have made minor formatting changes to a few of the outputs in this column.) The numbers to the left of each line were produced by the profiler; they tell how many times the line was executed. They show, for instance, that main was called once, it tested 999 integers, and found 168 primes. Function prime was called 999 times. It returned one 168 times and returned zero the other 831 times (a reassuring quick check: 168+831=999). It tested a total of 78,022 potential factors, or about 78 factors for each number examined for primality.

Program P1 is correct but slow. On a VAX-11/750 it computes all primes less than 1000 in a couple of seconds, but requires three minutes to find those less than 10,000. Profiles of those computations show that most of the time is spent testing factors. The next program therefore considers as potential factors of *n* only those integers up to $\sqrt{n}$. The integer function root converts its integer argument to floating point, calls the library function sqrt, then converts the floating-point answer back to an integer. Program P2 contains the two old functions and the new function root:

```
        int root(int n)
5456    { return (int) sqrt((float) n); }

        int prime(int n)
        {    int i;
999          for (i = 2; i <= root(n); i++)
5288             if (n % i == 0)
831                  return 0;
168          return 1;
        }

        main()
        {    int i, n;
1            n = 1000;
1            for (i = 2; i <= n; i++)
999              if (prime(i))
168                  printf("%d\n", i);
        }
```

The change was evidently effective: the line counts in Program P2 show that only 5288 factors were tested (a factor of 14 fewer than in Program P1). A total of 5456 calls were made to root: divisibility was tested 5288 times, and the loop terminated 168 times because i exceeded root(n). But even though the counts are greatly reduced, Program P2 runs in 5.8 seconds, while P1 runs in just 2.4 seconds (a table at the end of this section contains more details on run times). What gives?

So far we have seen only *line-count* profiles. A *procedure-time* profile gives fewer details about the flow of control but more insight into CPU time:

%time	cumsecs	#call	ms/call	name
82.7	4.77			_sqrt
4.5	5.03	999	0.26	_prime
4.3	5.28	5456	0.05	_root
2.6	5.43			_frexp
1.4	5.51			_doprnt
1.2	5.57			_write
0.9	5.63			mcount
0.6	5.66			_creat
0.6	5.69			_printf
0.4	5.72	1	25.00	_main
0.3	5.73			_close
0.3	5.75			_exit
0.3	5.77			_isatty

The procedures are listed in decreasing order of run time. The time is displayed both in cumulative seconds and as a percent of the total. The three procedures in the source program, main, prime and root, were compiled to record the number of times they were called. It is encouraging to see the same counts once again. The other procedures are unprofiled library routines that perform miscellaneous input/output and housekeeping functions. The fourth column tells the average number of milliseconds per call for all functions with statement counts.

The procedure-time profile shows that sqrt uses the lion's share of CPU time. It was called 5456 times, once for each test of the for loop. Program P3 calls that expensive routine just once per call of prime by moving the call out of the loop:

```
           int prime(int n)
           {     int i, bound;
999              bound = root(n);
999              for (i = 2; i <= bound; i++)
5288                  if (n % i == 0)
831                       return 0;
168              return 1;
           }
```

Program P3 is about 4 times as fast as P2 when *n*=1000 and over 10 times as fast when *n*=100,000. At *n*=100,000, the procedure-time profile shows that sqrt takes 88 percent of the time of P2, but just 48 percent of the time of P3. It is a lot better, but still the cycle hog.

Program P4 incorporates two additional speedups. First, it avoids almost three-quarters of the square roots by special checks for divisibility by 2, 3, and 5. The statement counts show that divisibility by two identifies roughly half the inputs as composites, divisibility by three gets a third of the remainder, and divisibility by five catches a fifth of those numbers still surviving. Second, it avoids about half the remaining divisibility tests by considering only odd numbers as potential factors. It is faster than P3 by a factor of about three, but

it is also buggier than its predecessor. Here is (buggy) Program P4; can you
spot the problem by examining the statement counts?

```
          int root(int n)
265       {    return (int) sqrt((float) n); }

          int prime(int n)
          {    int i, bound;
999            if (n % 2 == 0)
500                return 0;
499            if (n % 3 == 0)
167                return 0;
332            if (n % 5 == 0)
67                 return 0;
265            bound = root(n);
265            for (i = 7; i <= bound; i = i+2)
1530               if (n % i == 0)
100                    return 0;
165            return 1;
          }

          main()
          {    int i, n;
1              n = 1000;
1              for (i = 2; i <= n; i++)
999                if (prime(i))
165                    printf("%d\n", i);
          }
```

The previous programs found 168 primes, while P4 found just 165. Where
are the three missing primes? Sure enough, I treated three numbers as special
cases, and introduced one bug with each: `prime` reports that 2 is not a prime
because it is divisible by 2, and similarly botches 3 and 5. The tests are
correctly written as

```
if (n % 2 == 0)
    return (n == 2);
```

and so on. If n is divisible by 2, it returns 1 if n is 2, and 0 otherwise. The
procedure-time profiles of Program P4 are summarized in this table for
$n = 1000$, 10,000, and 100,000:

N	PERCENT OF TIME IN		
	sqrt	prime	other
1000	45	19	36
10,000	39	42	19
100,000	31	56	13

Program P5 is faster than P4 and has the additional benefit of being correct. It replaces the expensive square root operation with a multiplication, as shown in this fragment:

```
265             for (i = 7; i*i <= n; i = i+2)
1530                if (n % i == 0)
100                     return 0;
165             return 1;
```

It also incorporates the correct tests for divisibility by 2, 3, and 5. The total speedup is about twenty percent over P5.

The final program tests for divisibility only by integers that have previously been identified as primes; Program P6 is in Section 1.4, coded in the Awk language. The procedure-time profile of the C implementation shows that at $n=1000$, 49 percent of the run time is in prime and main (the rest is in input/output), while at $n=100,000$, 88 percent of the run time is spent in those two procedures.

This table summarizes the programs we've seen. It includes two other programs as benchmarks. Program Q1 computes primes using the Sieve of Eratosthenes program in Solution 2. Program Q2 measures input/output cost. For $n=1000$, it prints the integers 1, 2, ..., 168; for general n, it prints the integers 1, 2, ..., $P(n)$, where $P(n)$ is the number of primes less than n.

PROGRAM	RUN TIME IN SECONDS, N=		
	1000	10,000	100,000
P1. Simple version	2.4	169	?
P2. Test only up to root	5.8	124	2850
P3. Compute root once	1.4	15	192
P4. Special case 2, 3, 5	0.5	5.7	78
P5. Replace root by *	0.3	3.5	64
P6. Test only primes	0.3	3.3	47
Q1. Simple sieve	0.2	1.2	10 4
Q2. Print 1..$P(n)$	0.1	0.7	5.3

This section has concentrated on one use of profiling: as you're tuning the performance of a single subroutine or function, profilers can show you where the run time is spent.

1.2 Using Profilers

Profilers are handy for small programs, but indispensable for working on large software. Brian Kernighan used a line-count profiler on the 4000-line C program that interprets programs written in the Awk programming language. At that time the Awk interpreter had been widely used for several years. Scanning the 75-page listing showed that most counts were hundreds and thousands, while a few were tens of thousands. An obscure piece of initialization code, though, had a count near a million. Kernighan changed a few parts of the six-line loop, and thereby doubled the speed of the program. He never would have guessed the hot spot of the program, but the profiler led him right to it.

Kernighan's experience is quite typical. In a paper cited under Further Reading, Don Knuth presents an empirical study of many aspects of Fortran programs, including their profiles. That paper is the source of the often quoted (and more often misquoted) statement that, "Less than 4 per cent of a program generally accounts for more than half of its running time." Numerous studies on many languages and systems have shown that for most programs that aren't I/O-bound, a large fraction of the run time is spent in a small fraction of the code. This pattern is the basis of testimonials like the following:

> In his paper, Knuth describes how the line-count profiler was applied to itself. The profile showed that half of the run time was spent in two loops. Changing a few lines of code doubled the speed of the profiler in less than an hour's work.

> Column 14 describes how profiling showed that a thousand-line program spent eighty percent of its time in a five-line routine. Rewriting the routine with a dozen lines doubled the speed of the program.

> In 1984 Tom Szymanski of Bell Labs put an intended speedup into a large system, only to see it run ten percent slower. He started to remove the modification, but then enabled a few more profiling options to see why it had failed. He found that the space had increased by a factor of twenty; line counts showed that storage was allocated many more times than it was freed. A single instruction fixed that bug. The correct implementation sped the system up by a factor of two.

> Profiling showed that half of an operating system's time was spent in a loop of just a few instructions. Rewriting the loop in microcode made it an order of magnitude faster but didn't change the system's throughput: the performance group had optimized the system's idle loop!

These experiences raise a problem that we only glimpsed in the last section: on what inputs should one profile a program? The primality programs had the single input n, which nonetheless strongly affects the time profile: input/output dominates for small n, while computation dominates for large n. Some programs have profiles quite insensitive to the input data. I'd guess that most payroll programs have pretty consistent profiles, at least from February to November. The profiles of other programs vary dramatically with the input. Haven't you ever suspected that your system was tuned to run like the wind on the manufacturer's benchmark, while it crawls like a snail on your important jobs? Take care in selecting your input mix.

Profilers are useful for tasks beyond performance. In the primality exercise, they pointed out a bug in Program P4. Line counts are invaluable for evaluating test coverage; zero counts, for instance, show untested code. Dick Sites of

Digital Equipment Corporation describes other uses of profiling: "(1) Deciding what microcode to put on chip in a two-level microstore implementation. (2) A friend at Bell Northern Research implemented statement counts one weekend in a real-time phone switching software system with multiple asynchronous tasks. By looking at the unusual counts, he found six bugs in the field-installed code, all of which involved interactions between different tasks. One of the six they had been trying (unsuccessfully) to track down via conventional debugging techniques, and the others were not yet identified as problems (i.e., they may have occurred, but nobody could attribute the error syndrome to a specific software bug)."

1.3 A Specialized Profiler

The principles of profiling we've seen so far apply to languages ranging from assemblers and Fortran to Ada. But many programmers now work in more powerful notations. How should we profile a computation in Lisp or APL, or in a network or database language?

We'll take UNIX pipelines as an example of a more interesting computational model. Pipelines are a sequence of filters; data is transformed as it flows through each filter. This classic pipeline prints the 25 most common words in a document, in decreasing frequency.†

```
cat $* |
tr -cs A-Za-z '\012' |
tr A-Z a-z |
sort |
uniq -c |
sort -r -n |
sed 25q
```

I profiled the pipeline as it found the 25 most common words in a book of about 60,000 words. The first six lines in the output were:

```
3463 the
1855 a
1556 of
1374 to
1166 in
1104 and
   . . .
```

---

† The seven filters perform the following tasks: (1) Concatenate all input files. (2) Make one-word lines by transliterating the complement (-c) of the alphabet into newlines (ASCII octal 12) and squeezing out (-s) multiple newlines. (3) Transliterate upper case to lower case. (4) Sort to bring identical words together. (5) Replace each run of duplicate words with a single representative and its count (-c). (6) Sort in reverse (-r) numeric (-n) order. (7) Pass through a stream editor; quit (q) after printing 25 lines. Section 10.5 uses a picture to describe the sort | uniq -c | sort idiom in steps 4, 5 and 6.

Here is the "pipeline profile" of the computation on a VAX-11/750:

lines	words	chars	times	
10717	59701	342233		
57652	57651	304894	14.4u 2.3s 18r	tr -cs A-Za-z \012
57652	57651	304894	11.9u 2.2s 15r	tr A-Z a-z
57652	57651	304894	104.9u 7.5s 123r	sort
4731	9461	61830	24.5u 1.6s 27r	uniq -c
4731	9461	61830	27.0u 1.6s 31r	sort -rn
25	50	209	0.0u 0.2s 0r	sed 25q

The left parts describe the data at each stage: the number of lines, words, and characters. The right parts describe the filters between the data stages: user, system, and real times in seconds are followed by the command itself.

This profile provides much information of interest to programmers. The pipeline is fast; 3.5 minutes of real time for 150 book pages is moving right along. The first sort consumes 57 percent of the run time of the pipeline; that finely tuned utility will be hard to speed up further. The second sort takes only 14 percent of the pipeline's time, but is ripe for tuning.† The profile also identifies a little bug lurking in the pipeline. UNIX gurus may enjoy finding where the null line was introduced.

The profile also teaches us about the words in the document. There were 57651 total words, but only 4731 distinct words. After the first transliteration program, there are 4.3 letters per word. The output showed that the most common word was "the"; it accounts for 6 percent of the words in the files. The six most common words account for 18 percent of the words in the file. Special-casing the 100 most common words in English might speed things up. Try finding other interesting factoids in the counts.

Like many UNIX users, I had previously profiled pipelines by hand, using the word count (wc) command to measure files and the time command to measure processes. A "pipeline profiler" automates that task. It takes as input the names of a pipeline and several input files, and produces the profile as output. Two hours of my time and fifty lines of code sufficed to build the profiler. The next section elaborates on this topic.

1.4 Building Profilers

Building a real profiler is hard work. Peter Weinberger built the C line-count profiler that produced the output we saw earlier; the project took him several weeks of effort spread over several months. This section describes how a simple version can be built more easily.

Dick Sites claimed that his friend "implemented statement counts one

---

† The second sort takes 25 percent of the run time of the first sort on just 8 percent of the number of input lines — the numeric (-n) flag is expensive. When I profiled this pipeline on a single column, the second sort was almost as expensive as the first; the profile is sensitive to the input data.

weekend". I found that pretty hard to believe, so I decided I'd try to build a profiler for Awk, an unprofiled language that is described in Appendix 1. A couple of hours later, my profiler produced this output when I ran the Awk version of Program P6:

```
BEGIN {  <<<1>>>
    n = 1000
    x[0] = 2; xc = 1
    print 2
    for (i = 3; i <= n; i++) {  <<<998>>>
        if (prime(i)) {  <<<167>>>
            print i
        }
    }
    exit
}

function prime(n,  i) {  <<<998>>>
    for (i=0; x[i]*x[i]<=n; i++) {  <<<2801>>>
        if (n % x[i] == 0) {  <<<831>>>
            return 0
        }
    }
    {  <<<167>>>  }
    x[xc++] = n
    return 1
}
```

The number in angle brackets after a left curly brace tells how many times the block was executed. Fortunately, the counts match those produced by the C line counter.

My profiler consists of two five-line Awk programs. The first program reads the Awk source program and writes a new program in which a distinct counter is incremented at the start of each block and a new END action (see Appendix 1) writes all counts to a file at the end of execution. When the resulting program runs, it produces a file of counts. The second program reads those counts and merges them back into the source text. The profiled program is about 25 percent slower than the original, and not all Awk programs are handled correctly — I had to make one-line changes to profile several programs. But for all its flaws, a couple of hours was a small investment to get a prototype profiler up and running. Section 7.2 of *The AWK Programming Language* cited in Section 2.6 presents details on a similar Awk profiler.

Quick profilers are more commonly written than written about. Here are a few examples:

In the August 1983 *BYTE*, Leas and Wintz describe a profiler implemented as a 20-line program in 6800 assembly language.

Howard Trickey of Bell Labs implemented function counts in Lisp in an hour by changing defun to increment a counter as each function is entered.

In 1978, Rob Pike implemented a time profiler in 20 lines of Fortran. After `CALL PROFIL( 10 )`, subsequent CPU time is charged to counter 10.

On these and many other systems it is possible to write a profiler in an evening. The resulting profiler could easily save you more than an evening's work the first time you use it.

1.5 Principles

This column has only scratched the surface of profiling. I've stuck to the basics, and ignored exotic ways of collecting data (such as hardware monitors) and exotic displays (such as animation systems). The message of the column is equally basic:

Use a Profiler. Make this month Profiler Month. Please profile at least one piece of code in the next few weeks, and encourage your buddies to do likewise. Remember, a programmer never stands as tall as when stooping to help a small program.

Build a Profiler. If you don't have a profiler handy, fake it. Most systems provide basic profiling operations. Programmers who had to read console lights 25 years ago can get the same information today from a graphics window on a personal workstation. A little program is often sufficient to package a system's instrumentation features into a convenient tool.

1.6 Problems

1. Suppose the array $X[1..1000]$ is sprinkled with random real numbers. This routine computes the minimum and maximum values:

```
Max := Min := X[1]
for I := 2 to 1000 do
    if X[I] > Max then Max := X[I]
    if X[I] < Min then Min := X[I]
```

   Mr. B. C. Dull observed that if an element is a new maximum, then it cannot be a minimum. He therefore rewrote the two comparisons as

```
if      X[I] > Max then Max := X[I]
else if X[I] < Min then Min := X[I]
```

   How many comparisons will this save, on the average? First guess the answer, then implement and profile the program to find out. How was your guess?

2. The following problems deal with computing prime numbers.

   a. Programs P1 through P6 squeezed two orders of magnitude out of the run time. Can you wring any more performance out of this approach to the problem?

   b. Implement a simple Sieve of Eratosthenes for computing all primes less than n. The primary data structure for the program is an array of n bits, all initially true. As each prime is discovered, all of its multiples in the array are set to false. The next prime is the next true bit in the array.

c. What is the run time as a function of n of the sieve in part b? Find an algorithm with running time of $O(n)$.

d. Given a very large integer (say, several hundred bits), how would you test it for primality?

3. A simple statement-count profiler increments a counter at each statement. Describe how to decrease memory and run time by making do with fewer counters. (I once used a Pascal system in which profiling a program slowed it down by a factor of 100; the line-count profiler described in this column uses tricks like this to slow down a program by only a few percent.)

4. A simple procedure-time profiler estimates the time spent in each procedure by observing the program counter at a regular interval (60 times a second on my system). This information tells the time spent in each part of the program text, but it does not tell which procedures called the time hogs. Some profilers give the cost of each function and its dynamic descendants. Show how to gather more information from the runtime stack to allocate time among callers and callees. Given this data, how can you display it in a useful form?

5. Precise numbers are useful for interpreting profiles of a program on a single data set. When there is a lot of data, though, the volume of digits can hide the message in the numbers. How would you display the profiles of a program or a pipeline on 100 different inputs? Consider especially graphical displays of the data.

6. Program P6 in Section 1.4 is a correct program that is hard to prove correct. What is the problem, and how can you solve it?

1.7 Further Reading

Don Knuth's "Empirical Study of Fortran Programs" appeared in volume 1 of *Software—Practice and Experience* in 1971 (pp. 105–133). Section 3 on "dynamic statistics" discusses both line-count and procedure-time profilers, and the statistics they were used to gather. Section 4 tunes seventeen critical inner loops, for speedup factors ranging from 1.5 to 13.1. I have read this classic paper at least once a year for the past decade, and it gets better every time. I strongly recommend it.

COLUMN 2: **ASSOCIATIVE ARRAYS**

Anthropologists say that language has a profound effect on world view. That observation, usually known as Whorf's hypothesis, is often summarized as "Man's thought is shaped by his tongue."

Like most programmers, my computing thought is shaped by my Algol-like tongue. PL/1, C and Pascal look pretty much alike to programmers like me, and it's not hard for us to translate such code into Cobol or Fortran. Our old, comfortable thought patterns can be easily expressed in these languages.

But other languages challenge the way we think about computing. We are amazed by Lispers as they work magic with their S-expressions and recursion, by APL fans who model the universe as the outer product of a couple of long vectors, and by Snobol programmers who seem to turn any problem into a big string. We Algolish programmers may find it painful to study these foreign cultures, but the exposure usually yields insight.

This column is about a language feature outside the Algol heritage: associative arrays. The arrays we know have numeric subscripts, while associative arrays permit references like *count* ["cat"]. Such data structures are present in languages such as Snobol and Rexx (an IBM command interpreter); they allow complex algorithms to be expressed in simple programs. These arrays are close enough to Algol to be understood quickly, yet novel enough to challenge our thinking habits.

This column examines the associative arrays provided by the Awk language. Most of Awk is from the Algol tradition, but its associative arrays and several other features merit study. The next section introduces Awk's associative arrays. Subsequent sections describe two substantial programs that are cumbersome in most Algol-like languages, yet can be elegantly expressed in Awk.

2.1 Associative Arrays in Awk

The Awk language is sketched in Appendix 1. We'll review the language briefly by studying a program to find suspicious entries in a file of names. Each line in the program is a "pattern-action" pair. For each input line that matches a pattern on the left, the action enclosed in brackets on the right is executed.

The complete Awk program contains only three lines of code:

```
length($1) > 10 { e++; print "long name in line", NR}
NF != 1         { e++; print "bad name count in line", NR}
END             { if (e > 0) print "total errors: ", e }
```

The first pattern catches long names. If the first field (named $1) is longer than 10 characters, then the action increments e and prints a warning using the builtin variable NR (for number of record, or line number). The variable e counts errors; Awk conveniently initializes all variables to zero. The second pair catches lines that do not contain exactly one name (the builtin variable NF counts the number of fields in the input line). The third action is executed at the end of the input. It prints the number of errors, if there were any.

Associative arrays aren't at Awk's core; many Awk programs don't use them. But the arrays are integrated nicely into the language: like other variables, they aren't declared and are automatically initialized at their first use.

We'll now turn to a second problem on names: given a file of n names, we are to generate all n^2 pairs of names. I know several people who have used such a program in selecting first and middle names for their children. If the input file contains the names Billy, Bob and Willy, the output might lead parents to a euphonic selection such as Billy Bob and away from Billy Willy.

This program uses the variable n to count the number of names seen so far. Like all Awk variables, it is initially zero. The first statement is executed for each line in the input; note that n is incremented before it is used.

```
    { name[++n] = $1 }
END { for (i = 1; i <= n; i++)
          for (j = 1; j <= n; j++)
              print name[i], name[j]
    }
```

After the input file has been read, the names have been stored in *name*[1] through *name*[n]. The END action prints the pairs with two for loops. Although this program uses only numeric subscripts,† note that it doesn't have to declare the size of the *name* array.

The program generates a lot of output, especially if some names occur several times in the input file. The next program therefore uses an array indexed by strings to clean the input file. Here is the complete program:

```
{ if (count[$1]++ == 0) print $1 }
```

When a name is first read its *count* is zero, so the name is printed and the array element is incremented. When subsequent occurrences of the name are read, its

---

† Snobol distinguishes between *arrays* that have numeric subscripts and *tables* whose subscripts are strings. Awk has only one kind of array; numeric subscripts are converted to strings before they are stored. Subscripts may have multiple indices — Awk creates a single key by concatenating the indices, separated by a special character.

count is larger and no further action is taken. At the end of the program the
subscripts of *count* represent exactly the set of names.

That fact allows us to combine the two previous programs into one: given a
file of (possibly duplicated) names, this program prints all unique pairs.

```
      { name[$1] = 1 }
END { for (i in name)
           for (j in name)
                print i, j
      }
```

The associative array *name* represents the set of names. All values in *name* are
1; the information is contained in the array indices. That information is
retrieved by a loop of the form

```
      for (i in name) statement
```

The loop iterates `statement` over all values *i* that are a subscript of *name*,
which are exactly the names in the input file. The loop enumerates all names,
but in an arbitrary order; the names will usually not be sorted. (Awk does provide a convenient interface to the UNIX system sort, but that's beyond the
scope of this column.)

The next program moves from the nursery to the kitchen. We would prefer
that a shopping list like

```
chips    3
dip      2
chips    1
cola     5
dip      1
```

be collapsed to the more convenient form

```
dip      3
cola     5
chips    4
```

This program does the job.

```
      { count[$1] = count[$1] + $2 }
END { for (i in count) print i, count[i] }
```

Section 1.3 describes a program for counting the number of times each word
occurs in a document. The following program does the job using Awk's fields as
an overly simple definition of words: a sequence of characters separated by
blanks. The strings "Words", "words" and "words;" are therefore three
different words.

```
      { for (i = 1; i <= NF; i++) count[$i]++ }
END { for (i in count) print count[i], i }
```

The program took 40 seconds of VAX-11/750 CPU time to process the 4500
words in a draft of this column. The three most frequent words were "the"

(213 occurrences), "to" (110) and "of" (104). We will return to the run time of this program in Section 11.1.

This trivial spelling checker reports all words in the input file that aren't in the dictionary file `dict`. The preprocessing uses Awk's `getline` command to read the dictionary into the array *goodwords*:

```
BEGIN { while (getline <"dict") goodwords[$1] = 1 }
      { for (i = 1; i <= NF; i++)
            if (!($i in goodwords))
                badwords[$i] = 1
      }
END   { for (i in badwords) print i }
```

The main processing collects *badwords*, and postprocessing prints the violations. The test

```
if ($i in goodwords) ...
```

evaluates to true if the ith field is a subscript of the *goodwords* array, and the not operator `!` negates the condition. A programmer unfamiliar with Awk might have used the simpler test

```
if (goodwords[$i] == 0) ...
```

That test yields the same answer but has the undesired side-effect of inserting a new zero-valued element into *goodwords*; many excess elements could dramatically increase the time and space requirements of the program.

With these small examples as background, we'll move on to two larger problems. Fortunately, we won't have to study much larger programs.

2.2 A Finite State Machine Simulator

Finite State Machines (FSMs) are an elegant mathematical model of computation and a useful practical tool. They arise in such diverse applications as the lexical analysis of programming languages, communication protocols, and simple hardware devices. Wulf, Shaw, Hilfinger and Flon cover the subject in Section 1.1 of their *Fundamental Structures of Computer Science* (published in 1981 by Addison-Wesley).

As an illustration, they consider the simple task of "suppressing" the starting ones in a stream of bits:

```
Input:  011010111
Output: 001000011
```

A one immediately following a zero is changed to a zero, and all other bits in the input stream are left unchanged.

The following two-state machine encodes the last input bit in its state: "LIZ" means "Last Input Zero" and "LIO" means "Last Input One".

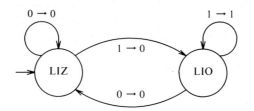

The arrow pointing at LIZ means that the machine starts in that state. The arc from LIZ to LIO says that if the machine is in LIZ and the input is a one, then the output is a zero and the next state is LIO.

The program that executes FSMs uses two primary data structures. If the FSM contains the arc

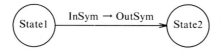

then the following equalities hold

```
trans[State1, InSym]  == State2
out[State1, InSym]    == OutSym
```

The name `trans` is for state transition and `out` is for output symbol.

The machine and input described above are encoded as follows.

```
LIZ 0 LIZ 0
LIZ 1 LIO 0
LIO 0 LIZ 0
LIO 1 LIO 1
start LIZ
0
1
1
0
  . . .
```

The first four lines represent the four edges of the FSM. The first line says that if the machine is in state LIZ and the input is zero, then the next state is LIZ and the output is zero. The fifth line identifies the start state, and subsequent lines are input data.

This program executes FSMs described in the above form.

```
run == 1 { print out[s, $1]; s = trans[s, $1] }
run == 0 { if ($1 == "start") { run = 1; s = $2 }
           else { trans[$1, $2] = $3; out[$1, $2] = $4 }
         }
```

The program has two primary modes. It starts with the variable *run* at the value zero. In that mode it adds machine transitions to the *trans* and *out* arrays. When the first field of a line is the string "start", the program stores the desired start state in *s* and switches to run mode. Each execution step then produces output and changes state as a function of the current input ($1) and the current state (*s*).

This miniature program has many flaws. Its response to undefined transitions, for instance, is catastrophic. The program as it stands is fit, at best, for personal use. On the other hand, it provides a convenient base upon which one might build a more robust program; see Problem 2.

2.3 Topological Sorting

The input to a topological sorting algorithm is a directed graph with no cycles, such as

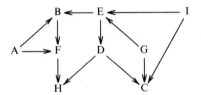

If the graph contains an edge from *A* to *B*, then *A* is *B*'s predecessor and *B* is *A*'s successor. The algorithm must order the nodes such that all predecessors appear before their successors; here is one of many possible orderings.

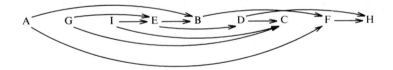

The algorithm must cope with the possibility that the input graph contains a cycle and therefore cannot be sorted.

Such an algorithm might be used, for instance, in drawing a three-dimensional scene of objects. Object *A* precedes object *B* if *B* is in front of *A* in the view, because *A* must be drawn before *B*. The scene of four rectangles on the left induces the partial order on the right.

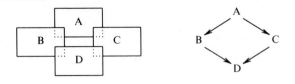

There are two valid orderings of the vertices: *A B C D* and *A C B D*. Each of the orderings properly overlays the objects. Other applications of topological sorting include laying out a technical document (terms must be defined before they are used) and processing hierarchical VLSI designs (an algorithm must process the components of a part before processing the part itself). Before reading on, think for a minute about how you would write a program for topologically sorting a directed graph.

We'll study a topological sorting algorithm from Section 2.2.3 of Knuth's *Art of Computer Programming, volume 1: Fundamental Algorithms*. The iterative step of the algorithm can be viewed as follows: choose a node *T* with no predecessors, write *T* to the output file, and then remove from the graph all edges emanating from *T*. This figure shows the algorithm's progress on the four-node scene graph. The stages are depicted from left to right; at each stage, the node *T* is circled.

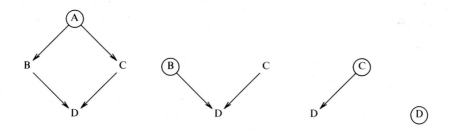

The resulting list is *A B C D*.

A slow implementation of this algorithm scans the entire graph at each step to find a node with no predecessors. We will now study a simpler algorithm that is also more efficient. For each node the algorithm stores the number of predecessors the node has and the set of its successors. For instance, the four-node graph drawn above is represented as:

NODE	PREDECESSOR COUNT	SUCCESSORS
A	0	B C
B	1	D
C	1	D
D	2	

The iterative step of the algorithm chooses a node whose predecessor count is zero, writes it on the output, and decrements the predecessor count of all its successors. It must be careful, though, to remember the order in which the counts went to zero; it uses a queue of nodes for that task. (If the queue becomes empty before all nodes have a predecessor count of zero, then the program reports that the graph contains a cycle.)

This pseudocode assumes that the graph is presented to the program as a sequence of (predecessor, successor) pairs, one pair per line.

```
as each (pred, succ) pair is read
    increment pred count of succ
    append succ to successors of pred
at the end of the input file
    initialize queue to empty
    for each node i
        if pred count of i is zero then append i to queue
    while queue isn't empty do
        delete t from front of queue; print t
        for each successor s of t
            decrement pred count of s
            if that goes to zero then append x to queue
    if some nodes were not output then report a cycle
```

The running time of the algorithm is proportional to the number of edges in the graph, which is within a constant factor of optimal. (Each edge is processed twice: once as it is read and once as it is removed from the queue.)

The Awk program implements the queue as an array with indices in the range $1..n$. The integer qlo is the index of the first element in the queue and qhi is the index of the last. The successor sets are implemented by two arrays. If A has the successors B, C and D, then the following relations hold

```
succct["A"] == 3
succlist["A", "1"] == "B"
succlist["A", "2"] == "C"
succlist["A", "3"] == "D"
```

The input to this Awk program is a file of predecessor, successor pairs. Its output is either the sorted node list or a warning that such a list doesn't exist.

```
    { ++predct[$2]                # record nodes in predct,
      predct[$1] = predct[$1]     # even those with no preds
      succlist[$1, ++succcnt[$1]] = $2
    }
END { qlo = 1
      for (i in predct) {
          n++; if (predct[i] == 0) q[++qhi] = i
      }
      while (qlo <= qhi) {
          t = q[qlo++]; print t
          for (i = 1; i <= succcnt[t]; i++) {
              s = succlist[t, i]
              if (--predct[s] == 0) q[++qhi] = s
          }
      }
      if (qhi != n) print "tsort error: cycle in input"
    }
```

The second line in the program ensures that all nodes occur as indices in *predct*, even those with no predecessors.

The associative arrays in this program represent several different abstract data types: a symbol table of node names, an array of records, a two-dimensional sequence of successor sets, and a queue of nodes. The small size of this program makes it easy to understand, but failing to distinguish abstract data types in a larger program could make it indecipherable.

2.4 Principles

Awk programmers can do a lot with a little. Most programs we've seen would be an order of magnitude larger in a conventional language. And the size reduction is due to just a few Awk features: implicit iteration over input lines, automatic separation into fields, initialization and conversion of variables, and associative arrays.

Those arrays are the only mechanism Awk has for combining its primitive data types of strings and numbers. Fortunately, associative arrays can represent many data structures quite naturally.

Arrays. One-dimensional, multidimensional and sparse arrays are all straightforward to implement.

Sequential Structures. Queues and stacks result from an associative array and an index or two.

Symbol Tables. Symbol tables provide a mapping from a name to a value. An Awk symbol table maintains *symtab* [*name*] = *value*. If all names have the same value, then the array represents a set.

Graphs. Finite State Machines and topological sort both process directed graphs. The FSM program uses a matrix representation for the graph, while topological sort uses an edge-sequence representation.

Education aside, of what practical value are Awk and its associative arrays? Awk programs are small. That's not always an advantage (like APL one-liners, they can be obnoxiously impenetrable), but ten lines of code is almost always better than a hundred. Unfortunately, Awk code tends to run slowly. Its symbol tables are relatively efficient, but arrays indexed by integers are orders of magnitude slower than the conventional implementation. When are small, slow programs useful?

The run-time cost of many programs is negligible compared to their development cost. The Awk topological sorting program is near production quality for some tasks; it should be more robust in the presence of errors.

Simple programs make useful prototypes. Let the users try a small program first. If they like it, build an industrial-strength version later.

I use Awk as a testing environment for subtle subroutines; we'll return to this topic in the next column.

2.5 Problems

1. Choose an Awk program in this column and rewrite it in a different language. How do the two programs compare in size of source code and run-time efficiency?

2. Enhance the FSM simulator in various ways. Consider adding error checking (bad states, bad inputs, etc.), default transitions, and character classes (such as integers and letters). Write a program to perform lexical analysis for a simple programming language.

3. The topological sorting program in the column reports the existence of a cycle if one is present. Modify it to print the cycle itself. Make it more robust in the presence of errors.

4. Show that a graph induced by a three-dimensional scene can contain cycles. Give restrictions that guarantee the absence of cycles.

5. Design programs for the following tasks. How can you use associative arrays to simplify the programs?

   a. *Trees.* Write a program to build and traverse binary trees.

   b. *Graphs.* Rewrite the topological sorting program using depth-first search. Given a directed graph and a distinguished node x, report all nodes that can be reached from x. Given a weighted graph and two nodes x and y, report the shortest path from x to y.

   c. *Documents.* Use a simple dictionary to transliterate from one natural language to another (a line in an English-French dictionary might contain the two words "hello bonjour"). Prepare a cross-reference listing of a text or program file, with all references to each word listed by line number. Awk programmers might try using input field separators and substitution commands to achieve a more realistic definition of words.

   d. *Random Sentence Generation.* The input to this program is a context-free grammar such as

         S → NP VP
         NP → AL N | N
         N → John | Mary
         AL → A | A AL
         A → Big | Little | Tiny
         VP → V AvL
         V → runs | walks
         AvL → Av | AvL Av
         Av → quickly | slowly

   The program should generate random sentences like "John walks quickly" and "Big Little Mary runs slowly quickly slowly".

   e. *Filters.* The second "name" program filters out duplicate words from a file; the spelling checker filters out words that are in the dictionary. Write other word filters, such as removing words that are not on an "approved list", but leaving approved words in the same order. (These tasks are easier when the inputs are sorted.)

f. *Board Games.* Implement Conway's "Game of Life". You might use Awk's `delete x[i]` statement to remove old board positions.

6. Describe various implementations of associative arrays, and analyze the access time and storage cost of each.

2.6 Further Reading

Aho, Kernighan, and Weinberger designed and built the original Awk language in 1977. (Whatever you do, don't permute the initials of their last names!) They describe the current language and its tasteful use in *The AWK Programming Language*, published by Addison-Wesley in 1988. Chapter 7 of their book shows how Awk is a useful tool for experimenting with algorithms; we will use Awk for that purpose in Columns 3, 13 and 14. Chapter 6 describes Awk as a processor for little languages; we'll use Awk for that purpose in Column 9. Other chapters provide a tutorial and reference manual and apply Awk to problems in data processing, databases and word processing. The Awk book is an excellent introduction to an interesting and useful language.

COLUMN 3: **CONFESSIONS OF A CODER**

Most programmers spend a lot of time testing and debugging, but those activities don't often get much attention in writing. This column describes how I tested and debugged a few hard subroutines, with an emphasis on the *scaffolding* I used in the process. The scaffolding around a building provides access to components that workers couldn't otherwise reach. Software scaffolding consists of temporary programs and data that give programmers access to system components. The scaffolding isn't delivered to the customer, but it is indispensable during testing and debugging.

Enough background, and on to two painful stories.

Confession 1. Several years ago I needed a selection routine in the middle of a 500-line program. Because I knew the problem was hard, I copied a 20-line subroutine from an excellent algorithms text. The program usually ran correctly, but failed every now and then. After two days of debugging, I tracked the bug down to the selection routine. During most of the debugging, that routine was above suspicion: I was convinced by the book's informal proof of the routine's correctness, and I had checked my code several times to make sure it matched the book. Unfortunately, a "<" in the book should have been a "≤". I was a little upset with the authors, but a lot madder at myself: fifteen minutes worth of scaffolding around the selection routine would have displayed the bug, yet I wasted two days on it.

Confession 2. Several weeks before I first wrote this column I was working on a book of my own, which included a selection routine. I used techniques of program verification to derive the code, so I was sure it was correct. After I placed the routine in the text, I wondered whether it was even worth my time to test it. I hemmed and hawed, trying to decide....

The conclusion and another confession come later in this column.

This column is about the testing and debugging tools I use on subtle algorithms. We'll start by scrutinizing two subroutines, complete with several common bugs to make our study more interesting. As a reward for plowing through all the code, this column concludes by describing a little subroutine library and some tests of its correctness; I hope that the library will make it easy for you to use correct versions of these routines in your programs.

> ## Warning — Buggy Code Ahead

3.1 Binary Search

The "black box" approach is at one extreme of testing: without knowing the structure of the program, hence viewing it as a black box, the tester presents a series of inputs and analyzes the output for correctness. This section is about a testing approach at the opposite extreme: the code is in a white box,† and we watch it as it works.

The code we'll study is a binary search. Here is the routine, together with a simple testbed:

```
function bsearch(t,   l, u, m) {
    l = 1; u = n
    while (l <= u) {
        m = int((l+u)/2)
print "   ", l, m, u
        if       (x[m] < t) l = m
        else if (x[m] > t) u = m
        else return m
    }
    return 0
}
$1=="fill"    { n = $2; for (i = 1; i <= n; i++) x[i] = 10*i }
$1=="n"       { n = $2 }
$1=="x"       { x[$2] = $3 }
$1=="print"   { for (i = 1; i <= n; i++) print i ":\t" x[i] }
$1=="search"  { t = bsearch($2); print "result:", t }
```

The Awk binary search function has the single argument t; later elements in the parameter list are the local variables. It should return an index of t in $x[1..n]$ if t is present in the array, and zero otherwise. The print statement traces the values of l, m and u throughout the search (the lower end, middle, and upper end of the current range). I indicate that it is scaffolding by placing it in the left margin. Can you spot any problems with the code?

The bottom five lines of the program are Awk "pattern-action" pairs. If the input typed by the user matches the pattern on the left, then the code within brackets on the right is executed. The pattern in the first pair is true if the first field of the input line typed by the user ($1) is fill. On such lines, the number in the second field ($2) is assigned to the variable n, and the for loop fills n values of the array x.

---

† Logic dictates that the boxes should be "opaque" and "transparent" ("painted" and "glass"?), but I'll stick with the traditional and illogical black and white.

Here's a transcript of a run of the program. I first typed `fill 5`, and the program created a sorted array of five elements. When I typed `print`, the program printed the contents of the array.

```
fill 5
print
1:          10
2:          20
3:          30
4:          40
5:          50
```

Now come a few searches in that array. I typed `search 10`, and the next three lines show the range narrowing to find that 10 is in position 1 in x. The searches for 40 and 30 are also correct.

```
search 10
    1 3 5
    1 2 3
    1 1 2
result: 1
search 40
    1 3 5
    3 4 5
result: 4
search 30
    1 3 5
result: 3
```

Unfortunately, the next search runs into trouble.

```
search 50
    1 3 5
    3 4 5
    4 4 5
    4 4 5
    4 4 5
    4 4 5
    4 4 5
    4 4 5
    . . .
```

With this clue, can you find the bug in the program?

Binary search is supposed to narrow the range $l..u$ until termination. The assignment `l=m` usually does so, but when l and m are equal it loops endlessly. The assignment should instead be `l=m+1`, which excludes m from the range. (The techniques of program verification help one derive this code systematically; excluding m is the key point in the proof of termination.) The assignment `u=m` should similarly be changed to `u=m-1`. The resulting correct binary search is in Appendix 2.

The n and x commands allow us to alter the arrays produced by `fill`. To find how the correct code behaves on a two-element array with equal elements, the command x 2 10 sets $x[2]$ to 10, and the next command sets n to 2.

```
fill 5
x 2 10
n 2
print
1:         10
2:         10
search 20
   1 1 2
   2 2 2
result: 0
```

The search for 20 then correctly reports that it is not in the array.

I'd be *really* surprised if someone shows me a bug in the final binary search program. I used program verification techniques to prove the code correct, and then I beat on it with the black-box test reproduced in Appendix 2. Simple observations like those described in this section reassure me that the code indeed behaves as I thought. That reassurance cost just six lines of Awk scaffolding beyond the binary search code.

The techniques of this section are simple and well known. Unfortunately, scaffolding is too often neglected by programmers. A few minutes spent testing a prototype of a subtle algorithm like binary search can save hours of debugging after it is incorporated in a large system. If a hard routine fails in a big program, construct scaffolding so you can access it directly, or better yet, build a small version in a supportive language like Awk.

3.2 Selection

The next program uses Hoare's algorithm to *select* the kth-smallest element of the array $x[1..n]$. Its job is to permute the elements of x so that $x[1..k-1] \leqslant x[k] \leqslant x[k+1..n]$. We will study this routine in detail in Column 15:

```
function select(l, u, k,    i, m) {
    if (l < u) {
        swap(l, l+int((u-l+1)*rand()))
        m = l
        for (i = l+1; i <= u; i++)
            if (x[i] < x[l])
                swap(++m, i)
        swap(l, m)
        if      (m < k) select(m+1, u, k)
        else if (m > k) select(l, m-1, k)
    }
}
```

The code was easy to prove correct; it passed all tests on the first try.

That program uses "tail recursion": the recursive call is the last statement in the procedure. Tail recursion can always be transformed to iteration by replacing subroutine calls by assignment and loop statements. The next version replaces the recursive routine with a `while` loop, and this returns us to my next confession. My first mistake, of course, was in debating whether to test the code. Any author who errs as often as I do should either test the program or label it with "WARNING — UNTESTED CODE". The second mistake is in the selection routine itself; any ideas?

```
function swap(i, j,  t) { t = x[i]; x[i] = x[j]; x[j] = t }
function select(k,  l, u, i, m) {
     l = 1; u = n
     while (l < u) {
print l, u
         swap(l, l+int((u-l+1)*rand()))
         m = l
comps = comps + u-1
         for (i = l+1; i <= u; i++)
             if (x[i] < x[l])
                 swap(++m, i)
         swap(l, m)
         if        (m < k) l = m+1
         else if (m > k) u = m-1
     }
}
$1=="fill"  { n = $2; for (i = 1; i <= n; i++) x[i] = rand() }
$1=="n"     { n = $2 }
$1=="x"     { x[$2] = $3 }
$1=="print" { for (i = 1; i <= n; i++) print "   ", x[i] }
$1=="sel"   { comps = 0; select($2); print "  compares:", comps
              print "  compares/n:", comps/n
              for (i=1;   i < k;  i++) if (x[i] > x[k]) print i
              for (i=k+1; i <= n; i++) if (x[i] < x[k]) print i
            }
```

We'll first watch the program at work. The `fill` command sprinkles random numbers in the range [0,1] into the array, and `print` is like that in the previous program.

```
fill 5
print
    0.93941
    0.532356
    0.392797
    0.446203
    0.535331
```

The command `sel 3` partitions the array so that the third-smallest element is in $x[3]$. It displays the computation as it progresses, and also checks the correctness of the final answer. The subsequent `print` command then displays the partitioned array.

```
sel 3
1 5
3 5
3 5
3 5
3 4
   compares: 11
   compares/n: 2.2
print
      0.446203
      0.392797
      0.532356
      0.535331
      0.93941
```

Although the code produces the correct answer, the trace is suspicious. Can you find the hint of the bug in that history?

We'll corner the bug in a more perverse array, built and displayed as follows.

```
fill 2
x 1 5
x 2 5
print
      5
      5
```

Selecting the second-smallest element works just fine, but there are problems in finding the smallest.

```
sel 2
1 2
   compares: 1
   compares/n: 0.5
sel 1
1 2
1 2
1 2
1 2
 . . .
```

With this information, it was easy for me to spot the bug and to handle the tail recursion more carefully; the final code is in Section 15.2 and Appendix 2. (The program computed many correct answers only because the bug was often hidden by the randomizing `swap` statement. Randomization, for better or worse, often compensates for bugs.)

Apart from its correctness problem, the original code has a "performance bug": even when it gives the right answer, it takes too long. We'll see in Column 15 that a correct selection program requires roughly $3.4n$ comparisons to find the median of an n-element array. These tests (and a dozen more like them) show that the performance of the correct selection routine from Appendix 2 is in the right ballpark:

```
fill 50
sel 25
   compares: 134
   compares/n: 2.68
fill 100
sel 50
   compares: 363
   compares/n: 3.63
```

I have removed the output of the `print` statements that traced the values of *l* and *u* to save space in this column; it was a pleasure to watch them behave properly as I conducted the real tests.

3.3 A Subroutine Library

Before this column was originally published in *Communications of the ACM*, many programmers had mentioned that they used pseudocode published in previous columns as a basis for implementing an algorithm in their favorite language. For some time I had wanted to collect the algorithms into a little library, but the code was always too long. When the Awk language acquired functions in early 1985, I realized that it was the ideal vehicle for communicating a set of useful subroutines in clean, succinct, and tested code.

The designer of an industrial-strength subroutine library must face the difficult problems of portability, efficiency, and general interfaces. The designer must also choose an implementation language, which gives programmers in that language easy access to the routines. Unfortunately, that choice usually denies the routines to users of other languages.

Appendix 2 is a set of "language-independent" subroutines, suitable for copying into various implementation languages. Since no sane programmer would code a serious application of this nature in Awk,† the code is equally useful to a programmer using any Algol-like language. The routines are short. Tradeoffs were made for brevity and against twenty- and thirty-percent improvements in efficiency. There are no interfaces; all routines operate on the array $x[1..n]$. These short, clean, correct routines provide a useful starting point for programmers without a better library.

The routines themselves are less than half the program text; the remainder is a black-box correctness test. (Scaffolding is often this big. In Chapter 13 of *The Mythical Man Month*, Fred Brooks states that there might be "half as much code in scaffolding as there is in product"; in Section 1.4.1 of

---

† Apart from sequential search and insertion sort, all subroutines in the library are designed for efficient asymptotic running times — usually $O(n \log n)$. For problems on arrays, the overhead of Awk's interpretation and associative arrays renders it orders of magnitude slower than conventional compiled languages.

Fundamental Algorithms Knuth raises that to as much scaffolding as delivered code.) The tests all have the same structure: an input is constructed, the routine is called, and the answer is then checked for correctness. The progress of the tests is reported as they are run. This is helpful for locating any error, and encouraging for the runs that report no errors — at least you know they did something. Most tests are run for all values of n in 0..*bign*, where *bign*=12; at most $O(n^3)$ work is performed at each value of n. The sorting test examines $n!$ random permutations for n in 0..*smalln*, where *smalln*=5. That gives a high probability of uncovering any permutation on which the algorithm fails. (Most random tests aren't so thorough.) The complete program required seven minutes of CPU time on a VAX-11/750.

With the exception of the selection routine discussed earlier (and described in detail in Column 15), I wrote the Awk routines by transliterating pseudocode published in previous columns. Those columns give informal correctness arguments using techniques of program verification. I had tested all the routines before publication, using a combination of watching, measuring and black-box testing; some columns report bugs I found during that process. I therefore wasn't surprised when testing uncovered no logical errors in the routines; I fixed a few syntax errors in less than a minute each.

Testing did, however, uncover two interesting bugs in Awk. The first manifested itself as an infinite loop in the binary search routine `bsearch`. When I extracted from Appendix 2 a tiny scaffolding program like the one in Section 3.1, the infinite loop was obvious. I presented the resulting fifteen lines to Brian Kernighan, who was adding several new features to Awk at that time. I was unsure of whether the bug was in my program or his, but hopeful enough that it might be Kernighan's fault to risk certain ridicule if the fault were mine. Changing the line

```
else return m
```

to

```
else { print "returning"; return m}
```

showed that the Awk interpreter's new functions had the common bug of not properly executing a `return` from within a loop. After the bug was identified, Kernighan fixed Awk within ten minutes.

I then ran back to my terminal to watch with glee as the test of binary search ran successfully for all n in the range 1..9. I was heartbroken to see the test fail for n=10. At that time, *bign*=10. Because I couldn't think of any good reason why code should fail at n=10, I re-ran the test with *bign*=9 and *bign*=11, hoping that the problem was in the last test. Unfortunately, the code consistently worked properly up through 9 and failed at 10 and 11. What changes between 9 and 10?

Awk variables can be either numbers or strings. The Awk manual states that if the two operands in a comparison are both numeric then they are compared as numbers, otherwise they are compared as strings. Because of unusual circumstances in this program involving function calls, the interpreter inappropriately observed that the string "10" precedes the string "5". I created a six-line program that tickled this bug, and Kernighan had the problem fixed the next day.

3.4 Principles

This column has touched on several tasks common in the programmer's day-to-day life. None is particularly glamorous, but all are important.

Scaffolding. This column illustrates prototype routines, print routines to observe program behavior, measurement code, and component tests. Other scaffolding includes test data (dummy files and data structures) and program "stubs" that facilitate top-down testing by simulating unfinished routines.

Special-Purpose Languages. The right language can make a program an order of magnitude shorter and cleaner. Exploit the strengths of the languages available to you. Awk is a fine language for prototyping algorithms: its associative arrays let you simulate many common data structures; its fields, implicit loops, and pattern-action pairs simplify input/output; implicit declaration and initialization of variables lead to succinct programs. Chapter 7 of *The AWK Programming Language* (cited in Section 2.6) presents more information on using Awk to experiment with algorithms. Section 13.2 and Solution 14.6 give Awk scaffolding for two subtle algorithms.

Testing and Debugging. This column concentrated on testing and debugging small components. White-box views of the computation initially show that the code behaves as we expected. Black-box tests are later used to increase our confidence in the correctness of the routine.

Bug Reports. The component test of the subroutine library inadvertently turned into a system test for Awk's recently added functions. Kernighan calls this the "new user phenomenon": each new user of a fresh system uncovers a new class of bugs. I pushed harder on functions than previous users. On the two occasions when the 300-line program tickled an Awk bug, I reproduced the bizarre behavior in a short program before reporting the problem (fifteen lines in one case, six in the other). Stu Feldman of Bell Communications Research speaks from years of experience maintaining a Fortran compiler:

> The program author, support organization, and your friends will all ignore you if you send a bug report and a 25,000 line program listing. It took me several years to teach [name changed to protect the guilty] this fact and get him to work on it. Techniques involve staring at code, intuition, bisection (try throwing out the last half of the subroutine), etc.

If you find a bug, report it with the smallest possible test case.

The Role of Program Verification. I need all the help I can get in making a correct program. Informal verification techniques help me write the code and check it before I ever implement it, and testing is crucial after I have the code in hand. Because I'm getting better at verification, I'm no longer astounded when a small but complex routine works the first time. If it doesn't work, I use testing and debugging to help me locate the invalid assertions and fix them along with the code (I'm usually able to resist those urges to "just change it until it works" — I try to write only programs that I understand). Appendix 2 illustrates two uses of assertions: the pre- and postconditions of a routine provide a precise and concise specification of its behavior, and assertion comments in the code (especially loop invariants) explain the algorithms. For a more direct application of verification ideas to testing, see Problem 3.

3.5 Problems

1. Build scaffolding that allows you to observe the behavior of routines in Appendix 2. Heaps are particularly interesting to watch.

2. Improve the `assert` routine of Appendix 2 so that it tells more about the location of the error.

3. The `assert` routine can also be used in white-box testing: change the assertions that are presently comments into calls to the assert routine. Rewrite assertions in that form for one of the routines in Appendix 2. Does that strengthen the tests in the sense of Problem 4?

4. Evaluate the quality of the black-box tests in Appendix 2 by introducing bugs into the various routines. Which bugs are caught by which tests?

5. Rewrite the programs in this column in another language. How long are they compared to the Awk code?

6. Write scaffolding that allows you to time the performance of various algorithms in Appendix 2. How can you present the results graphically?

7. Build a subroutine library like that in Appendix 2 for a different problem domain, such as graph algorithms. Strive for short, correct algorithms that are also reasonably efficient.

8. By the literal specifications in Appendix 2, this is a correct sorting algorithm:

    ```
    for (i = 1; i <= n; i++)
        x[i] = i;
    ```

    A sorting algorithm must, of course, also guarantee that the output array is a permutation of the input. The sorting, heap, and selection algorithms in Appendix 2 guarantee this property by altering the array only by using the `swap` routine. How would you test a less structured program for the permutation property?

COLUMN 4: **SELF-DESCRIBING DATA**

You just spent three CPU hours running a simulation to forecast your company's financial future, and your boss asks you to interpret the output:

```
Scenario 1:    3.2% -12.0%    1.1%
Scenario 2:   12.7%   0.8%    8.6%
Scenario 3:    1.6%  -8.3%    9.2%
```

Hmmm.

You dig through the program to find the meaning of each output variable. Good news — Scenario 2 paints a rosy picture for the next fiscal year. Now all you have to do is uncover the assumptions of each. Oops — the disaster in Scenario 1 is your company's current strategy, doomed to failure. What did Scenario 2 do that was so effective? Back to the program, trying to discover which input files each one reads....

Every programmer knows the frustration of trying to decipher mysterious data. The first two sections of this column discuss two techniques for embedding descriptions in data files. The third section then applies both methods to a concrete problem.

4.1 Name-Value Pairs

Many document production systems support bibliographic references in a form something like this:

```
%author     A. V. Aho
%author     M. J. Corasick
%title      Efficient string matching:
            an aid to bibliographic search
%journal    Communications of the ACM
%volume     18
%number     6
%month      June
%year       1975
%pages      333-340
```

```
%title      The Art of Computer Programming,
            Volume 3: Sorting and Searching
%author     D. E. Knuth
%publisher  Addison-Wesley
%city       Reading, Mass.
%year       1973
```

Blank lines separate entries in the file. A line that begins with a percent sign contains an identifying term followed by arbitrary text. Text may be continued on subsequent lines that do not start with a percent sign.

The lines in the bibliography file are *name-value pairs*: each line contains the name of an attribute followed by its value. The names and the values are sufficiently self-describing that I don't need to elaborate further on them. This format is particularly well-suited to bibliographies and other complex data models. It supports missing attributes (books have no volume number and journals have no city), multiple attributes (such as authors), and an arbitrary order of fields (one need not remember whether the volume number comes before or after the month).

Name-value pairs are useful in many databases. One might, for instance, describe the aircraft carrier *USS Nimitz* in a database of naval vessels with these pairs:

```
name         Nimitz
class        CVN
number       68
displacement 81600
length       1040
beam         134
draft        36.5
flightdeck   252
speed        30
officers     447
enlisted     5176
```

Such a record could be used for input, for storage, and for output. A user could prepare a record for entry into the database using a standard text editor. The database system could store records in exactly this form; we'll soon see a representation that is more space-efficient. The same record could be included in the answer to the query "What ships have a displacement of more than 75,000 tons?"

Name-value pairs offer several advantages for this hypothetical application. A single format can be used for input, storage, and output, which simplifies life for user and implementer alike. The application is inherently variable-format because different ships have different attributes: submarines have no flight decks and aircraft carriers have no submerged depth. Unfortunately, the example does not document the units in which the various quantities are expressed; we'll return to that shortly.

Some database systems store records on mass memory in exactly the form shown above. This format makes it particularly easy to add new fields to records in an existing database. The name-value format can be quite space-efficient, especially compared to fixed-format records that have many fields, most of which are usually empty. If storage is critical, however, then the database could be squeezed to a compressed format:

```
naNimitz¦clCVN¦nu68¦di81600¦le1040¦
be134¦dr36.5¦fl252¦sp30¦of447¦en5176
```

Each field begins with a two-character name and ends with a vertical bar. The input/output format and the stored format are connected by a data dictionary, which might start:

ABBR	NAME	UNITS
na	name	text
cl	class	text
nu	number	text
di	displacement	tons
le	length	feet
be	beam	feet
dr	draft	feet
fl	flightdeck	feet
sp	speed	knots
of	officers	personnel
en	enlisted	personnel

In this dictionary the abbreviations are always the first two characters of the name; that may not hold in general. Readers offended by hypocrisy may complain that the above data is not in a name-value format. The regular structure supports the tabular format, but observe that the header line is another kind of self-description embedded in the data.

Name-value pairs are a handy way to give input to any program. They are one of the tiniest of the "little languages" described in Column 9. They can help meet the criteria that Kernighan and Plauger propose in Chapter 5 of their *Elements of Programming Style* (the second edition was published by McGraw-Hill in 1978).

Use mnemonic input and output. Make input easy to prepare (and to prepare correctly). Echo the input and any defaults onto the output; make the output self-explanatory.

Name-value pairs can be very useful in code that is far removed from input-output. Suppose, for example, that we want to provide a subroutine that adds a ship to a database. Most languages denote the (formal) name of a parameter by its position in the parameter list. This positional notation can lead to remarkably clumsy calls:

```
addship("Nimitz", "CVN", "68", 81600, 1040,
        134, 36.5, 447, 5176,,,30,,,252,,,,)
```

The missing parameters denote fields not present in this record. Is 30 the speed

in knots or the draft in feet? A little discipline in commenting conventions
helps unravel the mess:

```
addship("Nimitz",  # name
        "CVN",     # class
        "68",      # number
        81600,     # disp
        1040,      # length
         ...)
```

Some languages support named parameters, which make the job easier:

```
addship(name = "Nimitz",
        class = "CVN",
        number = "68",
        disp = 81600,
        length = 1040,
         ...)
```

If your language doesn't have named parameters, you can simulate them with a
few routines (the variables name, class, etc., are distinct integers):

```
shipstart()
shipstr(name, "Nimitz")
shipstr(class, "CVN")
shipstr(number, "68")
shipnum(disp, 81600)
shipnum(length, 1040)
   ...
shipend()
```

4.2 Provenances in Programming

   The provenance of a museum piece lists the origin or source of the object.
Antiques are worth more when they have a provenance (this chair was built in
such-and-such, then purchased by so-and-so, etc.). You might think of a provenance as a pedigree for a non-living object.
   The idea of a provenance is old hat to many programmers. Some software
shops insist that the provenance of a program be kept in the source code itself:
in addition to other documentation in a module, the provenance gives the history
of the code (who changed what when, and why). The provenance of a data file
is often kept in an associated file (a transaction log, for instance). Frank
Starmer of Duke University tells how his programs produce data files that contain their own provenances:
   "We constantly face the problem of keeping track of our manipulations of
data. We typically explore data sets by setting up a UNIX pipeline like

```
sim.events -k 1.5 -l 3 |
sample -t .01 |
bins -t .01
```

The first program is a simulation with the two parameters k and 1 (set in this example to 1.5 and 3).† The vertical bar at the end of the first line pipes the output into the second program. That program samples the data at the designated frequency, and in turn pipes its output to the third program, which chops the input into bins suitable for graphical display as a histogram.

"When looking at the result of a computation like this, it is helpful to have an 'audit trail' of the various command lines and data files encountered. We therefore built a mechanism for 'commenting' the files so that when we review the output, everything is there on one display or piece of paper.

"We use several types of comments. An 'audit trail' line identifies a data file or a command-line transformation. A 'dictionary' line names the attributes in each column of the output. A 'frame separator' sets apart a group of sequential records associated with a common event. A 'note' allows us to place our remarks in the file. All comments begin with an exclamation mark and the type of the comment; other lines are passed through untouched and processed as data. Thus the output of the above pipeline might look like:

```
!trail sim.events -k 1.5 -1 3
!trail sample -t .01
!trail bins -t .01
!dict bin_bottom_value item_count
0.00    72
0.01    138
0.02    121
   ...
!note there is a cluster around 0.75
!frame
```

All programs in our library automatically copy existing comments from their input onto their output, and additionally add a new trail comment to document their own action. Programs that reformat data (such as bins) add a dict comment to describe the new format.

"We've done this in order to survive. This discipline aids in making both input and output data files self-documenting. Many other people have built similar mechanisms; wherever possible, I have copied their enhancements rather than having to figure out new ones myself."

Tom Duff of Bell Labs uses a similar strategy in a system for processing pictures. He has developed a large suite of UNIX programs that perform transformations on pictures. A picture file consists of text lines listing the commands that made the picture (terminated by a blank line) followed by the picture itself (represented in binary). The prelude provides a provenance of the picture. Before Duff started this practice he would sometimes find himself with a wonderful picture and no idea of what transformations produced it; now he can reconstruct any picture from its provenance.

---

† Note that the two parameters are set by a simple name-value mechanism. — J.B.

Duff implements the provenances in a single library routine that all programs call as they begin execution. The routine first copies the old command
lines to the output file and then writes the command line of the current program
on the output.

4.3 A Sorting Lab

To make the above ideas more concrete, we'll apply them to the task of conducting experiments on sort routines. Experiments in the last column dealt with
the correctness of the routines; these experiments concentrate on their run time.
This section will sketch an interface suitable for gathering performance data;
Column 15 uses such data. The input and output are both expressed in name-
value pairs, and the output contains a complete description of the input (its
provenance).

Experiments on sorting algorithms involve adjusting various parameters, executing the specified routine, then reporting key attributes of the computation.
The precise operations to be performed can be specified by a sequence of name-
value pairs. Thus the input file to the sorting lab might be this description of a
sorting experiment:

```
n          100000
input      identical
alg        quicksort
cutoff     10
partition  random
seed       379
```

In this example the problem size, n, is set to 100,000. The input array is initialized with identical elements (other options might include random, sorted,
or reversed elements). The sorting algorithm in this experiment is quick for
Quicksort; insert (for insertion sort) and heap (for Heapsort) might also be
available. The cutoff and partition names specify further parameters in
some implementations of quicksort.

The input to the simulation program is a sequence of experiments in the
above format, separated by blank lines. Its output is in exactly the same format
of name-value pairs, separated by blank lines. The first part of an output record
contains the original input description, which gives the provenance of each
experiment. The input is followed by three additional attributes: comps records
the number of comparisons made, swaps counts swaps, and cpu records the
run time of the procedure. An output record might therefore consist of the
input record shown above, together with these fields at the end:

```
comps      4772
swaps      4676
cpu        0.1083
```

Given the sort routines and the additional supporting procedures that do the real work, the control program is easy to build. Its main loop can be sketched in pseudocode as follows:

```
loop
    read input line into string S
    if end of file then break
    F1 := first field in S
    F2 := second field in S
    if S = "" then
        simulate()
        reset variables to their default values
    else if F1 = "n" then
        N := F2
    else if F1 = "alg" then
        if      F2 = "insertsort" then alg := 1
        else if F2 = "heapsort"   then alg := 2
        else if F2 = "quicksort"  then alg := 3
        else error("bad alg")
    else if F1 = "input" then
        ...
    write S on output
simulate()
```

The code reads each input line, processes the name-value pair, and copies it to the output. The `simulate()` routine performs the experiment and writes the output name-value pairs; it is called at each blank line and also at end of file.

This simple structure is useful for many simulation programs. Its output can be read by a human or fed to later programs. The input variables together provide a provenance of the experiment; because they appear with the output variables, any particular experiment can be repeated. The variable format allows additional input and output parameters to be added to future simulations without having to restructure existing data. Problem 8 shows how this approach can be used to perform sets of experiments.

4.4 Principles

This column has only scratched the surface of self-describing data. Some systems, for instance, allow a programmer to multiply two numeric objects of unspecified type (ranging from integers to arrays of complex numbers); at run time the system determines the types by inspecting descriptions stored with the operands, and then performs the appropriate action. Tagged-architecture machines provide hardware support of self-describing objects, and some communications protocols store data along with a description of its format and types. It is easy to give even more exotic examples of self-describing data.

This column has concentrated on two simple but useful kinds of self-descriptions. Each reflects an important principle of program documentation.

The most important documentation aid is a clean programming language. Name-value pairs are a simple, elegant, and useful linguistic mechanism.

The best place for program documentation is in the source file itself. A data file is a fine place to store its own provenance: it is easy to manipulate and hard to lose.

4.5 Problems

1. Self-documenting programs contain useful comments and suggestive indentation. Experiment with formatting a data file to make it easier to read. If necessary, modify the programs that process the file to ignore white space and comments. Start your task using a text editor. If the resulting formatted records are indeed easier to read, try writing a "pretty printing" program to present an arbitrary record in the format.

2. Give an example of a data file that contains a program to process itself.

3. The comments in good programs make them self-describing. The ultimate in a self-describing program, though, is one that prints exactly its source code when executed. Try to write such a program in your favorite language.

4. Many files are implicitly self-describing: although the operating system has no idea what they contain, a human reader can tell at a glance whether a file contains program source text, English text, numeric data, or binary data. How would you write a program to make an enlightened guess as to the type of such a file?

5. Give examples of name-value pairs in your computing environment.

6. Find a program with fixed-format input that you find hard to use, and modify it to read name-value pairs. Is it easier to modify the program directly or to write a new program that sits in front of the existing program?

7. Give examples of the general principle that the output of a program should be suitable for input to the program. For instance, if a program wants a date to be entered in the format "06/31/88", then it should not write:

```
Enter date (default 31 June 1988):
```

8. The text sketched how to do one experiment on a sorting algorithm. Often, though, experiments come in sets, with several parameters systematically varied. Construct a generator program that will convert this description

```
n          [100 300 1000 3000 10000]
input      [random identical sorted]
alg        quicksort
cutoff     [5 10 20 40]
partition  median-of-3
```

into $5 \times 3 \times 4 = 60$ different specifications, with each item in a bracket list expanded in the cross product. How would you add more complex iterators to the language, such as [from 10 to 130 by 20]?

9. How would you implement name-value pairs using Awk's associative arrays?

PART II: **TRICKS OF THE TRADE**

Here's a trick of the medical trade useful for anyone who donates blood. Before sticking the big needle in your arm, the nurse first pricks your finger for a few drops of blood. Some thoughtless nurses jab the pad of the index finger, which is the most sensitive spot of the most used finger. It is better to poke a less sensitive part (on the side, halfway down from nail to pad) of a less commonly used finger (the ring finger). This trick can make a blood donor's day a little more pleasant. Tell it to your friends before the next blood drive.

These columns describe some similar tricks of the programmer's trade. Column 5 is about finding simple solutions to hard problems, Column 6 is a collection of rules of thumb, and Column 7 describes quick calculations useful in computing. Column 8 is about managing large software projects; its trick is in helping a programmer in the trenches to see things from the boss's perspective.

You won't find a whole lot of code and mathematics here. These columns are at an intellectual level not far above the trick of drawing blood samples from the side of the ring finger. Fortunately, these tricks are almost as useful, and not too much harder to apply.

Column 5 appeared in the February 1986 *Communications of the ACM*, Column 6 appeared in March 1986, Column 7 appeared in September 1985, and Column 8 appeared in December 1987.

COLUMN 5: **CUTTING THE GORDIAN KNOT**

Gordius tied the knot. To the person who could untie it, Asia was the promised prize. For centuries the knot resisted all efforts, until Alexander the Great approached it in 333 B.C. Instead of repeating the vain efforts of his predecessors, he drew his sword and slashed through the knot; Asia was soon his. Since that time, "cutting the Gordian knot" has meant finding a clever solution to a complex problem.

In modern language, Alexander took the easy way out. This column is about taking the easy way out of programming problems.

A word about authenticity: with the exception of a few feeble (and, I hope, obvious) attempts at humor, all anecdotes in this column are true. Some names have been obscured to protect the guilty.

5.1 A Quiz

This quiz describes three problems that arose in real systems. The problems are classics: sorting, data transmission, and random numbers. You probably know some classic solutions, but try to find a more elegant approach before you peek at the solutions in the next section.

Problem 1 — Sorting. The circulation department at *Scientific American* receives thousands of letters every day. The lion's share falls into half a dozen major categories: payments of bills, renewals of subscriptions, response to direct mail promotions, and so forth. The mail must be sorted into these groups before it is processed by the data entry clerks. Describe schemes for sorting the mail.

Problem 2 — Data Transmission. This problem was faced by a group of engineers at Lockheed's Sunnyvale, California, plant in 1981. Their daily problem was to transmit about a dozen drawings produced by a Computer Aided Design (CAD) system in their plant to a test station about 25 miles away, in the mountains near Santa Cruz. An automobile courier service took over an hour for the one-way trip (due to traffic jams and mountain roads) and cost a hundred dollars per day. Propose alternative data transmission schemes and estimate the cost of each.

Problem 3 — Random Samples. One step in the sampling process of a public opinion polling firm was to draw a random subset from a printed list of precincts. Their manual solution required a boring hour with a table of random numbers. An alert employee suggested a program to which the user types a list of N precinct names (typically a few hundred) and an integer M (typically a few dozen); the program's output is a list of M of the precincts chosen at random. Is there a better solution?

5.2 Some Solutions

If this section were titled "Solutions" it might sound like I thought I knew *the* answers. Here are a few good answers, but I wouldn't be surprised if other solutions were even better.

Solution 1. A clerk could manually place each letter in one of several bins; an automated solution might use a letter-processing machine for the job. Those solutions are expensive, so the magazine has the Post Office do the job for them. They use a different post office box number for each of the major categories, and the mail is delivered in bundles corresponding to the categories. Each box costs about a hundred dollars per year, which is a tiny fraction of the annual salary of a clerk.

Solution 2. The Lockheed team first considered using an existing microwave link to transmit data between the two sites, but producing the drawings at the test station would have required an expensive printer. Their final solution was to draw the pictures at the main plant, photograph them, then send the 35mm film to the test station by carrier pigeon, where it was enlarged and printed on an existing microfilm viewer. The pigeon took just half the time and less than one percent the dollar cost of the car (the birds worked, literally, for pigeon feed). Over a 16-month period the pigeons transmitted hundreds of rolls of film and lost only two (because there are hawks in the area, the pigeons carried no classified data).

Solution 3. It is immoral for a person to type in hundreds of names only so that a computer can ignore most of them. I therefore wrote a program to which the user types two input integers, M and N. The program then prints a sorted list of M integers chosen at random in the range 1..N. For instance, if $M=5$ and $N=100$, the output list might be

        6   8   47   66   80

The user then counts through the 100 precincts in the list, and marks the numbers 6, 8, 47, 66 and 80 as selected. The resulting dozen-line program was easy to write and was eagerly used by the pollsters. We'll see programs for a similar task in Column 13.

When I talked about this problem at West Point, a cadet suggested an even better approach. To sample M precincts, photocopy the precinct list, cut the copy into equal-sized pieces with a paper slicer, vigorously shake the slips in a large paper bag, and then pull out M of them. That solution is rapid to implement and gives appropriately random answers, as long as you shake the bag hard enough.

5.3 Hints

In each story in the quiz, a simple insight made a hard problem easy. Here are a few ideas for you to ponder as you search for elegant solutions to hard problems that you face.

What the User Really Wants. An operations researcher was assigned to devise an elevator scheduling policy to minimize passenger waiting time in a certain building. After visiting the building, he realized that the problem his employer really wanted to solve was to minimize the discomfort to the passengers (who didn't enjoy waiting for elevators). He solved the problem by installing mirrors near each elevator. The passengers then spent their wait admiring themselves, and complaints about the speed of the elevators were dramatically reduced. He found what the users really wanted.

A slight variation of that trick is commonly used to make a slow program acceptable to its users. A microcomputer program I once wrote took two hours to process one thousand records, so at each record it printed a message like

```
Processing record 597 of 985
```

Because all records took roughly the same amount of time, the users could plan their schedules accordingly. I'm sure that the resulting program was more comfortable than a program twice as fast that didn't tell the user when it was going to finish. The users wanted predictability more than speed.

I once urged a company to replace their ugly seven-by-nine dot matrix printer with a handsome daisy wheel printer. The company rejected the idea out of hand: the current reports clearly had the authority of "The Computer", while attractive reports would look like some mere human had typed them. The users wanted authority, not beauty. With similar motivation, some compilers report that "this program contains 1 errors" to remind the user that computers are stupid.

Knowing what the user really wants doesn't always make life easier. If your specification is to ensure that

$$X[1] \leqslant X[2] \leqslant X[3] \leqslant \cdots \leqslant X[N]$$

you might use the simple program

```
for I := 1 to N do X[I] := I
```

or the even more elegant code

```
N := 0
```

If you know that the user really wants to sort the array, though, neither of these programs will prove particularly useful.

Costs and Benefits. Before settling on a solution, understand its costs and benefits. The benefits of excellent documentation are worth the cost of programmer time if the program is frequently used by many people; the costs far outweigh the benefits if the program is a one-shot job. Many jobs worth doing aren't worth doing right. A novelist is foolish to agonize over each word in a shopping list.

Most problems have many potential solutions. Consider, for instance, the problem of injuries suffered in automobile accidents. Accidents are avoided by measures such as driver training, strict enforcement of speed limits, stiff penalties for drunk driving, and a good system of public transportation. If accidents do occur, injuries can be reduced by the design of the passenger compartment, wearing seat belts, and air bags. And if injuries are suffered, their effect can be reduced by paramedics at the scene, helicopter ambulances, trauma centers, and corrective surgery. One should understand the costs and benefits of all approaches before spending too much money on any single approach.

Don't Make the Problem Too Hard. An old puzzle asks how a barometer can be used to compute the height of a building. Answers range from dropping the instrument from the top and measuring the time of its fall to giving it to the building's superintendent in return for a look at the plans. A modern version of the puzzle asks how a personal computer can balance a checkbook. An elegant solution is to sell the machine and deposit the money.

Peter Denning observes that many tasks that are commonly implemented on home computers can be done more effectively by hand: "It's much faster to look at my monthly calendar on the wall than to turn on the computer, insert a floppy, load it, start the calendar program, and read my appointments. The same comment applies to recipes. My bookkeeping system for papers I handle as an editor depends on a file drawer and simple looseleaf notebook. I can quickly keep track of the status of all papers, referees, revisions, etc. It is significantly faster than any of the computerized systems I've seen used by other editors. Putting my system on a computer would slow it down. I'm able to get my job done faster without a computer."

Computers provide excellent solutions to some hard problems, but they aren't the universal solvent. Clever programmers leave their swords at home and cut Gordian knots with pigeons, post offices, paper bags, or looseleaf notebooks.

Don't Make the Problem Too Easy. In his wonderful *How To Solve It*, Polya points out that "the more general problem may be easier to solve"; he calls this the Inventor's Paradox. It is possible to write a program to permute the values in the variables A through G such that

$$A \leqslant B \leqslant C \leqslant D \leqslant E \leqslant F \leqslant G$$

It is a lot easier, though, to copy the variables into an array X, call a general sorting routine, and then copy X back into the variables.

Use the Right Tools in the Right Way. When the house-spouse complained that he had just spent half an hour writing a note to the milkman, his kindly wife suggested that next time he write the note *before* he puts it in the bottle. The UNIX program `tr` transliterates all occurrences of certain characters in its input file to other characters in its output file. A colleague found the following program consuming enormous amounts of time on our system.

```
tr a A <input >temp1
tr b B <temp1 >temp2
tr c C <temp2 >temp1
   ...
tr z Z <temp1 >output
remove temp1 temp2
```

The programmer wanted to change all lower-case letters to upper case. He eventually did the job more simply and more efficiently with this command.

```
tr a-z A-Z <input >output
```

If a program seems too awkward, try to find a simpler solution.

What Do You Reward? Brilliance is typically the act of an individual, but incredible stupidity can usually be traced to an organization. A popular Western writer once confessed that when he was paid by the word, the heroes in his books always took six bullets to die. When programmers are paid by the line of code, how do you suppose the array $X[1..1000]$ is initialized to zero? (Hint: programmers paid by the speedup initially produce slow code, and programmers required to execute a certain percentage of branches during testing have a lot of statements of the form if true then ....)

A programmer friend who works for a large company had just shaved 25 percent from the run time of a program. He was ecstatic. The program consumed two hours per day of supercomputer time, and the ten-line change reduced that by half an hour, for a savings of several hundred dollars per day. He bubbled in to the computation center with the good news of an extra half hour per day on their biggest engine, and was surprised to see their crestfallen faces. Because of the company's internal billing policy, this change would cost the comp center roughly $100,000 per year in funny-money. That company's organizational structure actively discouraged effective utilization of a multi-million dollar resource.

We've Always Done it this Way. For twenty years the plant had faithfully put a small hole in a mass-produced flywheel. Drilling the hole was expensive, so the mechanical engineers investigated other ways of putting it there. The team finally asked why the hole was there, and refused to accept the pat answer of "it's always been there". They eventually found that the original prototype flywheel was a little out of balance, so the designer reduced the mass on the heavy side by drilling the hole. For two decades that quick fix left its legacy in slightly out-of-balance devices. The team's elegant solution of ignoring the hole was not only cheaper, it gave better flywheels.

It's frustrating enough that people don't look for new solutions because "we've always done it this way". It's even worse when management ignores your wonderful new solution because "we've never done it that way". (Some companies still use that excuse for building huge applications systems in assembly code rather than in a high-level language.) Good luck in getting past this mindset, but beware the power of your enemy. The bureaucracy at a large university was explained as, "This school is two hundred years old and has never done anything for the first time."

Profit from Play. As a college freshman I had just learned about binary search and about assembly language coding. For my own amusement, and as an excuse for learning a little more about both subjects, I implemented a general-purpose binary search routine in assembly language. I had a part-time job in the data-processing center, and a few weeks later a run was cancelled after the operators estimated it would take two hours. We found that the bulk of the time was devoted to a sequential search, and when we replaced that with a call to my subroutine the run finished in ten minutes.

Dozens of times since then I have seen today's toy turn into next week's beast of burden or next year's product. In the September 1985 *Scientific American*, Kee Dewdney describes the atmosphere at Bell Labs in which it is impossible to draw the line between work and play. (My management even considers writing these columns as work, when it is about the most fun I can imagine.) One colleague, for instance, spent a week developing a color-graphics system because he wanted to draw pictures of a robot doing a back-flip. A few months later a chemist used the system to illustrate the structure of a molecule. The metallic spheroids that were bodily parts for the robot served as atoms in the molecule. The result was well worth the few minutes required to apply existing tools to the new task, and easily justified the cost of building the system in the first place.

5.4 Principles

Most of the stories in this column have the same outline: a hero was too lazy to solve a problem the hard way, and found an easy way out. Bob Martin said it best: "Attack the problem, not the programming."

5.5 Problems

1. I was once asked to write a program to transmit one particular data set from one personal computer to another PC of a very different architecture. A few questions showed that the file had only 400 records of 20 numeric digits each. How would you proceed?

2. When a new researcher reported to work for Thomas Edison, Edison asked him to compute the volume of a light bulb. After several hours with calipers and calculus, the new guy returned with the answer of 150 cubic centimeters. In less than a minute, Edison computed and responded "Closer to 155." What was Edison's insight?

3. To conduct an experiment, a psychologist needed to produce random permutations of three observers and three stress levels (High, Medium, Low).

After discussing the problem, we agreed that a program should produce output like this:

```
1  3L  2M  1H
2  3H  1M  2L
3  1L  2H  3M
4  1M  2L  3H
   . . .
```

The first line describes subject number 1, who is to be seen first by observer 3 in a low stress level, then by observer 2 under medium stress, and finally by observer 1 under high stress.

When I first thought about the problem I quickly sketched a program. One six-element array contains the six permutations of $\{1,2,3\}$ and another contains the six permutations of $\{L,M,H\}$. The program randomly chooses one of each, and then prints the two permutations spliced together. How would you generate these random permutations? (Hint: what is a common way to randomly generate one object out of six?)

4. This code finds the closest point in the array $X[1..N]$ to the point B:

```
BestDist := Infinity
for I := 1 to N do
    ThisDist := sqrt((A[I].X - P.X)**2 + (A[I].Y - P.Y)**2)
    if ThisDist < BestDist then
        BestDist := ThisDist
        BestPoint := I
```

Statistics from Section 7.2 show that the sqrt routine is the time bottleneck of the routine. Find a way to make the code run faster.

5. Critique the following examples of problem solving.

   a. When two people were chased by a bear, one stopped to put on running shoes. "You dummy," said the second, "you can't outrun a bear." The first replied, "I don't have to outrun that bear, I just have to outrun you."

   b. *Problem:* What should you do if you are chased by a bear, and you don't know whether it is a black bear or a grizzly bear? *Solution:* Run up a tree. If it is a black bear, it will run up after you. But if it is a grizzly, it will just knock the tree down then walk over to get you.

5.6 Further Reading

Of the many books that discuss problem solving, my favorite is *Conceptual Blockbusting* by James L. Adams (second edition published by Norton in 1979). Adams defines conceptual blocks as "mental walls that block the problem-solver from correctly perceiving a problem or conceiving its solution". His excellent book encourages you to bust them.

One problem with all such books is that so much general problem solving divorced from any particular technical area begins to look like "just puzzles". I tried to remedy that in my book *Programming Pearls* (published by Addison-Wesley in 1986). It interweaves programming details with stories of finding the easy way out of some important, hard problems. See especially the index entries for common sense, conceptual blocks, elegance, engineering techniques, insight, Inventor's Paradox, problem definition, and simplicity.

5.7 Debugging *[Sidebar]*†

Every programmer knows that debugging is hard. Fortunately, there are often simple solutions to hard debugging problems. Debugging tasks range from designing tests that will flush out the little critters to repairing the broken pieces. We'll now focus on just one small part of the job: after we observe weird behavior, how do we identify the culprit who is causing the problem?

A great debugger makes the job look simple. Distraught programmers describe a bug that they've been chasing for hours, the master asks three or four questions, and three minutes later the programmers are pointing at the faulty code. The expert debugger never forgets that there has to be a logical explanation, no matter how mysterious the behavior may seem at the time.

That attitude is illustrated in an anecdote from IBM's Yorktown Heights Research Center. A programmer had recently installed a new computer terminal. All was fine when he was sitting down, but he couldn't log in to the system when he was standing up. That behavior was one hundred percent repeatable: he could always log in when sitting and never when standing.

Most of us just sit back and marvel at such a story. How could that darn terminal know whether the poor guy was sitting or standing? Good debuggers, though, know that there has to be a reason. Electrical theories are the easiest to hypothesize. Was there a loose wire under the carpet, or problems with static electricity? But electrical problems are rarely one-hundred-percent consistent. An alert IBMer finally asked the right question: how did the programmer log in when he was sitting and when he was standing? Hold your hands in front of you and try it yourself. The problem was in the terminal's keyboard: the tops of two keys were switched. When the programmer was seated he was a touch typist and the problem went unnoticed, but when he stood he was led astray by hunting and pecking.

At an ACM Chapter meeting in Chicago, I heard the story of a banking system written in APL that had worked for quite some time, but unexpectedly quit the first time it was used on international data. Programmers spent days scouring the code, but they couldn't find any stray command that would quit the program and return control to the operating system. When they observed the behavior more closely, they found that the problem occurred as they entered

---

† Sidebars in *Communications of the ACM* are offset from the text of the column, often in a bar at the side of the page. While they aren't an essential part of the column, they provide perspective on the material. In this book they appear as the last section in a column, marked as a "sidebar".

data for the country of Ecuador: when the user typed the name of the capital city (Quito), the program interpreted that as a request to quit the run!

In both cases the right questions would have guided a wise programmer to the bug in short order: "What do you do differently sitting and standing? May I watch you logging in each way?" "Precisely what did you type before the program quit?"

The best books I have seen on debugging are the two volumes of *The Medical Detectives* by Berton Roueché. The first volume was published in paperback by Washington Square Press in 1982, and the second volume appeared in 1986. The heroes in these books debug complex systems, ranging from mildly sick people to very sick towns. The problem-solving methods they use are directly applicable to debugging computer systems. These true stories are as spellbinding as any fiction.

COLUMN 6: **BUMPER-STICKER COMPUTER SCIENCE**

Every now and then, programmers have to convert units of time. If a program processes 100 records per second, for instance, how long will it take to process one million records? Dividing shows that the task takes 10,000 seconds, and there are 3600 seconds per hour, so the answer is about three hours.

But how many seconds are there in a year? If I tell you there are 3.155×10^7, you'll probably forget it. On the other hand, it is easy to remember that, to within half a percent,

> π seconds is a nanocentury.
>
> *Tom Duff*
> *Bell Labs*

So if your program takes 10^7 seconds, be prepared to wait four months.

The February 1985 column in *Communications of the ACM* solicited from readers bumper-sticker sized advice on computing. Some of the contributions aren't debatable: Duff's rule is a memorable statement of a handy constant. This rule about a program testing method (regression tests save old inputs and outputs to make sure the new outputs are the same) contains a number that isn't as ironclad,

> Regression testing cuts test intervals in half.
>
> *Larry Bernstein*
> *Bell Communications Research*

Bernstein's point remains whether the constant is 30% or 70%: these tests save development time.

There's a problem with advice that is even less quantitative. Everyone agrees that

> Absence makes the heart grow fonder.
>
> *Anon*

and

57

Out of sight, out of mind.

Anon

Everyone, that is, except the sayings themselves. There are similar contradic-
tions in the slogans in this column. Although there is some truth in each, all
should be taken with a grain of salt.

A word about credit. The name associated with a rule is usually the person
who sent me the rule, even if they in fact attributed it to their cousin Ralph
(sorry, Ralph). In a few cases I have listed an earlier reference, together with
the author's affiliation (as of September 1985, when this column first
appeared). I'm sure that I have slighted many people by denying them proper
attribution, and to them I offer the condolence that

Plagiarism is the sincerest form of flattery.

Anon

Without further ado, here's the advice, grouped into a few major categories.

6.1 Coding

When in doubt, use brute force.

Ken Thompson
Bell Labs

Avoid arc-sine and arc-cosine functions — you can usually do better
by applying a trig identity or computing a vector dot-product.

Jim Conyngham
Arvin/Calspan Advanced Technology Center

Allocate four digits for the year part of a date: a new millennium is
coming.

David Martin
Norristown, Pennsylvania

Avoid asymmetry.

Andy Huber
Data General Corporation

The sooner you start to code, the longer the program will take.

Roy Carlson
University of Wisconsin

If you can't write it down in English, you can't code it.

Peter Halpern
Brooklyn, New York

Details count.

Peter Weinberger
Bell Labs

If the code and the comments disagree, then both are probably wrong.

Norm Schryer
Bell Labs

If you have too many special cases, you are doing it wrong.

Craig Zerouni
Computer FX Ltd.
London, England

Get your data structures correct first, and the rest of the program will write itself.

David Jones
Assen, The Netherlands

6.2 User Interfaces

[The Principle of Least Astonishment] Make a user interface as consistent and as predictable as possible.

Contributed by several readers

A program designed for inputs from people is usually stressed beyond the breaking point by computer-generated inputs.

Dennis Ritchie
Bell Labs

Twenty percent of all input forms filled out by people contain bad data.

Vic Vyssotsky
Bell Labs

Eighty percent of all input forms ask questions they have no business asking.

Mike Garey
Bell Labs

Don't make the user provide information that the system already knows.

Rick Lemons
Cardinal Data Systems

For 80% of all data sets, 95% of the information can be seen in a good graph.

William S. Cleveland
Bell Labs

6.3 Debugging

Of all my programming bugs, 80% are syntax errors. Of the remaining 20%, 80% are trivial logical errors. Of the remaining 4%, 80% are pointer errors. And the remaining 0.8% are hard.

Marc Donner
IBM Watson Research Center

It takes three times the effort to find and fix bugs in system test than when done by the developer. It takes ten times the effort to find and fix bugs in the field than when done in system test. Therefore, insist on unit tests by the developer.

Larry Bernstein
Bell Communications Research

Don't debug standing up. It cuts your patience in half, and you need all you can muster.

Dave Storer
Cedar Rapids, Iowa

Don't get suckered in by the comments — they can be terribly misleading. Debug only the code.

Dave Storer
Cedar Rapids, Iowa

Testing can show the presence of bugs, but not their absence.

Edsger W. Dijkstra
University of Texas

Each new user of a new system uncovers a new class of bugs.

Brian Kernighan
Bell Labs

If it ain't broke, don't fix it.

Ronald Reagan
Santa Barbara, California

[The Maintainer's Motto] If we can't fix it, it ain't broke.

Lieutenant Colonel Walt Weir
United States Army

The first step in fixing a broken program is getting it to fail repeatably.

Tom Duff
Bell Labs

6.4 Performance

[The First Rule of Program Optimization] Don't do it.

[The Second Rule of Program Optimization — For experts only.] Don't do it yet.

Michael Jackson
Michael Jackson Systems Ltd.

The fastest algorithm can frequently be replaced by one that is almost as fast and much easier to understand.

Douglas W. Jones
University of Iowa

On some machines indirection is slower with displacement, so the most-used member of a structure or a record should be first.

Mike Morton
Boston, Massachusetts

In non-I/O-bound programs, less than four per cent of a program generally accounts for more than half of its running time.

Don Knuth
Stanford University

Before optimizing, use a profiler to locate the "hot spots" of the program.

Mike Morton
Boston, Massachusetts

[Conservation of Code Size] When you turn an ordinary page of code into just a handful of instructions for speed, expand the comments to keep the number of source lines constant.

Mike Morton
Boston, Massachusetts

If the programmer can simulate a construct faster than the compiler can implement the construct itself, then the compiler writer has blown it badly.

Guy L. Steele, Jr.
Tartan Laboratories

To speed up an I/O-bound program, begin by accounting for all I/O. Eliminate that which is unnecessary or redundant, and make the remaining as fast as possible.

> *David Martin*
> *Norristown, Pennsylvania*

The fastest I/O is no I/O.

> *Nils-Peter Nelson*
> *Bell Labs*

The cheapest, fastest and most reliable components of a computer system are those that aren't there.

> *Gordon Bell*
> *Encore Computer Corporation*

Most assembly languages have a loop operation that does a compare and branch in a single machine instruction; although it was intended for loops, it can sometimes be used to do a general comparison very efficiently.

> *Guy L. Steele, Jr.*
> *Tartan Laboratories*

[Compiler Writer's Motto — Optimization Pass] Making a wrong program worse is no sin.

> *Bill McKeeman*
> *Wang Institute*

Electricity travels a foot in a nanosecond.

> *Commodore Grace Murray Hopper*
> *United States Navy*

Lisp programmers know the value of everything but the cost of nothing.

> *Alan Perlis*
> *Yale University*

6.5 Documentation

[The Test of Negation] Don't include a sentence in documentation if its negation is obviously false.

> *Bob Martin*
> *AT&T Technologies*

When explaining a command, or language feature, or hardware widget, first describe the problem it is designed to solve.

David Martin
Norristown, Pennsylvania

[One Page Principle] A {specification, design, procedure, test plan} that will not fit on one page of 8.5-by-11 inch paper cannot be understood.

Mark Ardis
Wang Institute

The job's not over until the paperwork's done.

Anon

6.6 Managing Software

The structure of a system reflects the structure of the organization that built it.

Richard E. Fairley
Wang Institute

Don't keep doing what doesn't work.

Anon

[Rule of Credibility] The first 90% of the code accounts for the first 90% of the development time. The remaining 10% of the code accounts for the other 90% of the development time.

Tom Cargill
Bell Labs

Less than 10% of the code has to do with the ostensible purpose of the system; the rest deals with input-output, data validation, data structure maintenance, and other housekeeping.

Mary Shaw
Carnegie-Mellon University

Good judgement comes from experience, and experience comes from bad judgement.

Fred Brooks
University of North Carolina

Don't write a new program if one already does more or less what you want. And if you must write a program, use existing code to do as much of the work as possible.

Richard Hill
Hewlett-Packard S.A.
Geneva, Switzerland

Whenever possible, steal code.

Tom Duff
Bell Labs

Good customer relations double productivity.

Larry Bernstein
Bell Communications Research

Translating a working program to a new language or system takes ten percent of the original development time or manpower or cost.

Douglas W. Jones
University of Iowa

Don't use the computer to do things that can be done efficiently by hand.

Richard Hill
Hewlett-Packard S.A.
Geneva, Switzerland

Don't use hands to do things that can be done efficiently by the computer.

Tom Duff
Bell Labs

I'd rather write programs to write programs than write programs.

Dick Sites
Digital Equipment Corporation

[Brooks's Law of Prototypes] Plan to throw one away, you will anyhow.

Fred Brooks
University of North Carolina

If you plan to throw one away, you will throw away two.

Craig Zerouni
Computer FX Ltd.
London, England

Prototyping cuts the work to produce a system by 40%.

Larry Bernstein
Bell Communications Research

[Thompson's Rule for First-Time Telescope Makers.] It is faster to make a four-inch mirror then a six-inch mirror than to make a six-inch mirror.

Bill McKeeman
Wang Institute

Furious activity is no substitute for understanding.

H. H. Williams
Oakland, California

Always do the hard part first. If the hard part is impossible, why waste time on the easy part? Once the hard part is done, you're home free.

Always do the easy part first. What you think at first is the easy part often turns out to be the hard part. Once the easy part is done, you can concentrate all your efforts on the hard part.

Al Schapira
Bell Labs

6.7 Miscellaneous Rules

[Sturgeon's Law — This applies as well to computer science as to science fiction.] Sure, 90% of all software is crap. That's because 90% of everything is crap.

Mary Shaw
Carnegie-Mellon University

If you lie to the computer, it will get you.

Perry Farrar
Germantown, Maryland

If a system doesn't have to be reliable, it can do anything else.

H. H. Williams
Oakland, California

One person's constant is another person's variable.

Susan Gerhart
Microelectronics and Computer Technology Corporation

One person's data is another person's program.

Guy L. Steele, Jr.
Tartan Laboratories

[KISS] Keep it simple, stupid.

Anon

6.8 Principles

If you've made it this far, you'll certainly appreciate this excellent advice.

Eschew clever rules.

Joe Condon
Bell Labs

6.9 Problems

Although this column has allocated just a few words to each rule, most of the rules could be greatly expanded (say, into an undergraduate paper or into a bull session over a few beers). These problems show how one might expand the following rule.

Make it work first before you make it work fast.

Bruce Whiteside
Woodridge, Illinois

Your "assignment" is to expand other rules in a similar fashion.

1. Restate the rule to be more precise. The example rule might be intended as

   Ignore efficiency concerns until a program is known to be correct.

   or as

   If a program doesn't work, it doesn't matter how fast it runs; after all, the null program gives a wrong answer in no time at all.

2. Present small, concrete examples to support your rule. In Chapter 7 of their *Elements of Programming Style*, Kernighan and Plauger present ten tangled lines of code from a programming text. The convoluted code saved a single comparison, and incidentally introduced a minor bug. By "wasting" an extra comparison, they replace the code with two crystal-clear lines. With that object lesson fresh on the page, they present the rule

   Make it right before you make it faster.

3. Find "war stories" of how the rule has been used in larger programs.

   a. It is pleasant to see the rule save the day. Section 1.2, for instance, describes several examples when profiling a system pointed to hot spots which were then easily fixed.

   b. It can be even more impressive to hear how ignoring the rule leads to a disaster. When Vic Vyssotsky modified a Fortran compiler in the early 1960's he spent a week making a correct routine very fast, and thereby introduced a bug. The bug did not surface until two years later, because the routine *had never once been called* in over 100,000 compilations. Vyssotsky's week of premature optimization was worse than wasted: it made a good program bad. (This story, though, served as fine training for Vyssotsky and generations of Bell Labs programmers.)

4. Critique the rules. Which are always "capital-T Truth" and which are sometimes misleading? I once stated to Bill Wulf of Tartan Laboratories that "if a program doesn't work, it doesn't matter how fast it runs" as an undebatable fact. He raised the example of a document formatting program that we both used. Although the program was significantly faster than its predecessor, it could sometimes seem excruciatingly slow: it took several hours to compile a book. Wulf won our verbal battle with this argument: "Like all other large systems, that program today has ten documented, but minor, bugs. Next month, it will have ten different small, known bugs. If you could magically either remove the ten current bugs or speed up the program by a factor of ten, which would you pick?"

6.10 Further Reading

If you like heavy doses of unadorned rules, try Tom Parker's *Rules of Thumb* (Houghton Mifflin, 1983). The following rules appear on its cover:

   798. One ostrich egg will serve 24 people for brunch.

   886. A submarine will move through the water most efficiently if it is 10 to 13 times as long as it is wide.

The book contains 896 similar rules.

Many of Butler Lampson's "Hints for Computer System Design" in *IEEE Software 1*, 1 (January 1984) are handy rules of thumb:

   Handle normal and worst cases separately.

   In allocating resources, strive to avoid disaster rather than to attain an optimum.

Lampson's hints summarize his experience in building dozens of state-of-the-art hardware and software systems.

COLUMN 7: THE ENVELOPE IS BACK

Every programmer should feel comfortable with "back-of-the-envelope" calculations. When you're deciding whether to add a new command to a database system, for instance, you might want to estimate

How much programmer time is required to develop the code?

How many disks have to be added to store additional data?

Is the current CPU fast enough to provide reasonable response time?

Quick calculations are also useful in everyday life: will the reduced fuel bills of a 30-mile-per-gallon car balance a purchase price that is $1000 greater than a 20-mpg car?

I first described back-of-the-envelope calculations in the February 1984 *Communications of the ACM*. After that column appeared, many readers contributed further ideas on the topic. This column presents two of those: rules of thumb useful for programmers, and Little's Law (a simple rule of amazing utility). But before we get to the technical details, the next section provides some mental stretching exercises.

7.1 A Warm-Up for Cool Brains

The student told me that the run time of his binary search subroutine was $1.83 \log_2 N$. I asked, "1.83 what?" He thought for a few seconds while staring at the ceiling and the floor and finally responded, "Either microseconds or milliseconds — I'm not really sure."

The student was blissfully ignorant of a factor of one thousand, three orders of magnitude. He couldn't even offer the excuse that performance wasn't a concern — he cared enough to calculate three significant digits. Like too many programmers, the poor student suffered from what Douglas Hofstadter calls "number numbness": milliseconds and microseconds are both unimaginably small time units, so why bother distinguishing between the two? This section provides some resensitization exercises that are designed to increase your appreciation of orders of magnitude.

Is a factor of a thousand really such a big deal? A microyear is about 32

69

seconds while a milliyear is 8.8 hours — I deeply regret that I didn't let the student choose between those two for how long he had to stay after school. Electricity travels about a foot in a nanosecond — that's a bottleneck in supercomputer design. In a microsecond it can go across a large building, and in a millisecond from New York to Washington, D.C. And speaking of Washington, it seems that some people who live there are always forgetting the difference between a million and a billion.

A fast sprinter can run a hundred meters in ten seconds, for an average velocity of 10 meters per second. One thousand times that speed is faster than the space shuttle, while one-thousandth the rate is slower than an ant. A factor of a thousand *is* a big deal, but there are bigger deals yet. This table shows some additional order-of-magnitude checkpoints of velocity.†

METERS PER SECOND	ENGLISH EQUIVALENT	EXAMPLE
10^{-11}	1.2 in/century	Stalactites growing
10^{-10}	1.2 in/decade	Slow continent drifting
10^{-9}	1.2 in/year	Fingernails growing
10^{-8}	1 ft/year	Hair growing
10^{-7}	1 ft/month	Weeds growing
10^{-6}	3.4 in/day	Glacier
10^{-5}	1.4 in/hr	Minute hand of a watch
10^{-4}	1.2 ft/hour	Gastro-intestinal tract
10^{-3}	2 in/min	Snail
10^{-2}	2 ft/min	Ant
10^{-1}	20 ft/min	Giant tortoise
1	2.2 mi/hr	Human walk
10^{1}	22 mi/hour	Human sprint
10^{2}	220 mi/hour	Propeller airplane
10^{3}	37 mi/min	Fastest jet airplane
10^{4}	370 mi/min	Space shuttle
10^{5}	3700 mi/min	Meteor impacting earth
10^{6}	620 mi/sec	Earth in galactic orbit
10^{7}	6200 mi/sec	LA to satellite to NY
10^{8}	62,000 mi/sec	One-third speed of light

If I describe a moving object, you can probably estimate its velocity pretty accurately. Whether the object is a rocket flying through the air or a beaver gnawing through a log, you can most likely guess its speed to within a notch or two of its true position in the table. In the next section we'll work on intuition about computational velocity.

---

† The table was inspired by *Powers of Ten*, by Morrison *et al.* (published in 1982 by Scientific American Books). Its subtitle is "A book about the relative size of things in the universe and the effect of adding another zero". It zooms in 42 factors of ten from a view 10^{25} meters across (ten thousand times the diameter of our galaxy) to a view 10^{-16} meters across deep within a carbon atom.

7.2 Performance Rules of Thumb

I don't know how much salt costs, and I don't really care. It's so cheap that I use it without regard to cost, and when I run out I buy some more. Most programmers feel the same way about CPU cycles, with good reason — they cost next to nothing.

I expect that executives at salt companies have a different attitude toward the lowly substance. If each American consumes a dollar worth of salt each year, that creates a market worth a quarter of a billion dollars — a ten-percent decrease in production costs could be worth a fortune. And every now and then, programmers must worry about the cost of CPU cycles for a similar reason: some programs spend them by the billions.

The price of salt is usually marked on the container, but how can you determine the cost of a line of code? Benchmarking the performance of a computer system is a difficult and important task; multimillion-dollar systems are purchased on the basis of ten and twenty-percent differences. Fortunately, rough estimates are easier to come by. They may be off from their "true" values by a factor of two, but they're still useful.

I'll now describe how I spent half an hour to get ballpark cost estimates on the system I usually use, a VAX-11/750 running the C language and the UNIX operating system. (Even if you don't care about CPU time, you may be interested in the design of these simple experiments.) I started with a five-line C program whose guts were

```
n = 1000000;
for (i = 1; i <= n; i++)
    ;
```

The UNIX system's `time` command reported that it took 6.1 seconds. Each iteration of the null loop therefore cost 6.1 microseconds. My next experiment used the integer variables i1, i2 and i3:

```
n = 1000000;
for (i = 1; i <= n; i++)
    i1 = i2 + i3;
```

This code took 9.4 seconds, so an integer addition costs about 3.3 microseconds. To test the cost of procedure calls, I defined the function

```
int sum2(int a, int b)
{ return a+b; }
```

and assigned i1 := sum2(i2, i3) in the loop. That took 39.4 seconds, so a function call with two integer parameters takes about 30 microseconds.

Unfortunately, even experiments as simple as these are fraught with potential problems. Is C addition really as fast as 3.3 microseconds, or did the compiler notice that the same addition was done repeatedly and therefore perform it just once, before the loop? But if that happened, what else would account for the 3.3 microsecond delay? Maybe the new code was aligned differently in the instruction cache, or maybe the system was just busier during the second test. And so on and so on.

Testing those hypotheses expanded the performance experiments from a few minutes to half an hour, but I'm pretty sure that the resulting estimates are accurate to within, say, a factor of two. With that caveat, this table presents ballpark estimates of the cost of several mathematical operations in this implementation of C.

OPERATION	MICROSECONDS
Integer Operands	
Addition	3.3
Subtraction	3.7
Multiplication	10.6
Division	11.0
Floating Operands	
Addition	10.6
Subtraction	10.2
Multiplication	15.7
Division	15.7
Conversions	
Integer to float	8.2
Float to integer	11.2
Functions	
Sine	790
Logarithm	860
Square root	940

It's easy to summarize the data: most arithmetic operations in C cost about 10 microseconds. Integer addition/subtraction is faster (3.5 microseconds) and floating multiplication/division is slower (16 microseconds). But beware the evil functions! They're only a few characters to type, but they're two orders of magnitude more expensive than the other operators.

On those rare occasions when performance does matter, I use this data in two ways. The general trend helps me to make accurate estimates. If a routine performs N^2 steps of a few arithmetic operations each, a C implementation will take roughly half a minute when N is 1000. If the routine is called once a day, I won't worry about its efficiency from now on. If I had planned to call the routine several times a minute, though, I won't even bother coding it and instead search for a better solution.

The table also highlights the expensive operations. Budget-minded chefs can safely ignore the price of salt if caviar is on the menu; C programmers on this system can ignore the primitive arithmetic operations surrounding a square root. But beware that relative costs change from system to system. On a PDP-10 Pascal compiler I once used, floating point operations cost 2 microseconds, while square roots and integer-to-float conversions both cost 40 microseconds. A conversion in C costs 1 floating point operation while a square root costs 60; in

Pascal both costs are 20. Problem 2 encourages you to estimate the costs on your system.

7.3 Little's Law

Most back-of-the-envelope calculations use obvious rules: total cost is unit cost times number of units. Sometimes, though, one needs a more subtle insight. Bruce Weide of Ohio State University wrote the following note about a rule that is surprisingly versatile.

"The 'operational analysis' introduced by Denning and Buzen (see *Computing Surveys 10*, 3, November 1978, 225–261) is much more general than queueing network models of computer systems. Their exposition is excellent, but because of the article's limited focus, they didn't explore the generality of Little's Law. The proof methods have nothing to do with queues or with computer systems. Imagine *any* system in which things enter and leave. Little's Law states that 'The average number of things in the system is the product of the average rate at which things leave the system and the average time each one spends in the system.' (And if there is a gross 'flow balance' of things entering and leaving, the exit rate is also the entry rate.)

"I teach this technique of performance analysis in my computer architecture classes. But I try to emphasize that the result is a general law of systems theory, and can be applied to many other kinds of systems. For instance, if you're in line waiting to get into a popular nightspot, you might figure out how long you'll have to wait by standing there for a while and trying to estimate the rate at which people are entering. With Little's Law, though, you could reason, 'This place holds about 60 people, and the average Joe will be in there about 3 hours, so we're entering at the rate of about 20 people an hour. The line has 20 people in it, so that means we'll wait about an hour. Let's go home and read *Programming Pearls* instead.' You get the picture."

Peter Denning succinctly phrases this rule as "The average number of objects in a queue is the product of the entry rate and the average holding time." He applies it to his wine cellar: "I have 150 cases of wine in my basement and I consume (and purchase) 25 cases per year. How long do I hold each case? Little's Law tells me to divide 150 cases by 25 cases/year, which gives 6 years per case."

He then turns to more serious applications. "The response-time formula for a time-shared system can be proved using Little's Law and flow balance. Assume N terminals of average think time Z are connected to an arbitrary system with response time R. Each user cycles between thinking and waiting-for-response, so the total number of jobs in the meta-system (consisting of terminals and the computer system) is fixed at N. If you cut the path from the system's output to the terminals, you see a meta-system with average load N, average response time $Z+R$, and throughput X (measured in jobs per time unit). Little's Law says $N=X\times(Z+R)$, and solving for R gives $R = N/X - Z$."

Denning goes on to say that "Little's Law is more useful when augmented with the 'forced flow law' and the 'utilization law'. You can then calculate answers to questions like this: A humongous computer system contains a bazillion disks, a quadrillion CPUs, a classified operating system, and 20 terminals of average think time 20 seconds. Its disk unit is observed to serve 100 requests per job and runs at the rate of 25 requests per second. What is the system's throughput and response time? (I get 0.25 jobs/second and 60 seconds.) These answers are *exact* if the system is in flow balance, which is normally very close to true. *Any* system of arbitrary configuration containing a disk with those measured values and terminals of those measured values will have the same throughput and response time. Amazing? Only to the extent that one does not appreciate the power of the basic laws of system flow and congestion."

7.4 Principles

The three sections in this column highlight three assets that are often useful for programmers: familiarity with numbers, willingness to experiment, and mathematics, when you need it.

7.5 Problems

1. Make tables like the one in the first section to illustrate factors of ten in measures such as time, weight, distance, area and volume.

2. Conduct experiments to measure the performance of your computer system. Here is a starting list of useful quantities:

   > CPU Time
   >> Control flow: overhead of for, while, if, subroutine call
   >> Arithmetic operations
   >>> Integer/float: add, subtract, multiply, divide
   >>> Floating point: square root, logarithm, sine
   >>> Type conversions between integer and float
   >> String operations: comparison and copy
   > I/O Time
   >> Read/write one character/integer
   >> Disk access time, disk read time
   >> Disk accesses per database operation
   > Utilities
   >> Sort 10,000 integers in memory
   >> Sort 100,000 20-byte strings in a file
   >> Search a text file for a string

   Other handy facts include the speed of your compiler in lines of source code per second and the disk space required to store a one-byte file.

3. The data on run costs assumes a performance model in which variables are accessed in a constant amount of time and a given instruction always

requires the same amount of time to execute. Give examples of systems on which these and other "reasonable" assumptions are violated.

4. Estimate your city's death rate, measured in percent of population per year.

5. [P. J. Denning] Sketch a proof of Little's Law.

6. [P. J. Denning] Use Little's Law to characterize the flow of a job through a network of servers.

7. [B. W. Weide] Imagine a queue of customers waiting for service. In its usual interpretation, Little's Law relates the average total number of customers in the queue *and* in the server to the average time a customer spends waiting in the queue *and* in service. How are the average waiting time in the queue alone and the average number of customers in the queue alone related to these quantities?

8. [B. W. Weide] Many computer centers still have big mainframes that handle large numbers of batch jobs concurrently. Some even have a monitor showing the jobs awaiting execution, so you can see where your job stands. Jobs must await execution, of course, because there is always a backlog of work (this is due to Murphy's Law, not Little's). Suppose the average job spends 20 seconds "in execution" on a machine that can execute 10 jobs concurrently, and that your job is the last of 100 "awaiting execution" to be executed in first-in-first-out order. About how long can you expect to wait until your job is finished?

9. Determine various administrative costs in your organization. How much does it cost to buy a book beyond the cover price? To have a secretary type a letter? What is the cost of floor space, measured in dollars per square foot per year? What is the cost of telephone and computing systems?

7.6 Further Reading

Douglas Hofstadter's "Metamagical Themas" column in the May 1982 *Scientific American* is subtitled "Number numbness, or why innumeracy may be just as dangerous as illiteracy". It is reprinted with a postscript in his book *Metamagical Themas*, published by Basic Books in 1985.

7.7 Quick Calculations in Everyday Life *[Sidebar]*

Back-of-the-envelope calculations about everyday events are always good practice and good fun, and are sometimes even useful. A reader of a draft of this column described a trip to the supermarket he had taken a few days earlier. He kept a running total as he walked through the aisles by rounding each item to the nearest dollar. His final tally was $70.00, and he was confident enough to look at the register tape when the clerk announced the total price of $92.00. The clerk had mistakenly entered the product code of six oranges (number 429) as their price ($4.29); that raised a $2.00 purchase to $25.00.

Here's one that stumped me for a while: what is the volume of a typical 6-foot-tall male? (Volume refers to cubic centimeters of meat; cubic feet in a crowded elevator is another question entirely.) A common response figures that the typical male is 6 feet high by 2 feet wide by half a foot thick, for 6 cubic feet. A more accurate estimate exploits the fact that humans are roughly the same density as water, approximately 60 pounds per cubic foot (most swimmers float when they inhale and sink when they exhale). A person who weighs 180 pounds is therefore about 3 cubic feet. If you know a person's weight, this relation can give you their volume to within a few percent, a feat impossible by multiplying length by width by height.

Here are a few canned questions, but keep in mind that spontaneous questions are usually the most interesting.

1. If every person in your city threw a ping pong ball into your living room, how deep would the balls be?

2. What is the cost of a one-hour lecture at your organization? Include both preparation and audience time.

3. How much money will Americans spend this year on soft drinks? On cigarettes? On video games? On the space program?

4. How many words are in a typical book? How many words a minute do you read? How many words a minute do you type?

5. How many dollars per year is the difference between a 20-mile-per-gallon car and a 40 mpg car? Over the lifetime of a car? What if every driver in the United States chose one or the other?

6. How much does it cost to drive your car a mile? Don't forget insurance.

7. How much would it cost to buy extension cords to reach from the earth to the moon?

8. An old rule of thumb says that a human sitting in a room radiates about 100 watts. How many calories per day must supply that radiator?

I'd like to end with a plea to teachers. In his paper cited in Section 7.6, Hofstadter tells how he asked students in a New York City physics class the height of the Empire State Building, which they could see out the window. The true height is 1250 feet, but answers ranged from 50 feet to one mile. I recently had a similar experience *after* a lecture on "back-of-the-envelope" calculations. An examination question asked for the cost of a one-semester, fifteen-student class section at that college. Most students gave an answer within thirty percent of my estimate of $30,000, but the extremes ranged from a high of $100,000,000 to a low of $38.05.

If you're a teacher, spare ten minutes of lecture for this topic, then reinforce it with little examples throughout the class. Test your success by an examination question; I bet you'll find the answers interesting.

COLUMN 8: **THE FURBELOW MEMORANDUM**

A friend writes:

On several occasions I have heard you being outspokenly skeptical about the large budgets and staffs of certain development projects. While rummaging around for something else this morning I unearthed the attached document, which may help you understand the practical reasons why development projects operate as they do. It was written almost a decade ago by G. Furbelow, with whom Cadwallader-Cohen and I shared an office at the time. I obtained a copy to show to my boss, who remarked that he saw plenty of letters of this sort anyway, and didn't need any more.

In case you have forgotten, THESEUS-II is a communication system for the Defense Department, originally conceived for DOD in 1964 by a joint University-Industry Summer Study (Professor G, Manager V, and a six pack of Bud). It provides rapid-deployment hardened high capacity communications to connect any two points on the earth's surface; its basis is big drums of cable in low earth orbit. When DOD needs extra communications between, say, Zanzibar and the Persian Gulf, they pick an appropriately positioned cable drum and fire a retrorocket attached to one end of the cable. This causes the cable to unreel, reenter, and lay itself automatically, entrenching itself as it reaches the surface, so that only a direct nuclear hit will sever it once it's entrenched. Unfortunately, development and field testing problems have caused repeated delays in turnover of the system for operational use; even today most tests do not result in successful cable-laying. This problem is believed to be due to subtle flaws in the system control software. The system is expected to function as intended once these flaws are corrected.

At the time of Furbelow's letter his software staff was 368 people, and that turned out to be inadequate for completion of the task. By now the THESEUS-II software staff is 1850 people, and everyone concerned is optimistic that full operational status will soon be achieved.

8.1 The Memo

Date: September 13, 1978
Subject: 1979 Budget
From: G. Furbelow
To: J. R. Honcho

While I agree with you that my proposed 1979 budget increase to 229.3% of the 1978 budget seems unusually large, it is a standstill budget, which cannot be further reduced without serious impact on our committed work program. To make it clear how this situation comes about, I shall review the factors which led to the increase.

As you recall, our work program and work force were nearly static for several years prior to 1978. This year my organization undertook "catch-up" work on THESEUS-II, to reduce the backlog of deferred maintenance and enhancement requests. For this purpose we have an approved 1978 budget 6.8% higher than standstill. Our original staffing plan was to accommodate this work by adding 25 people to the staff on January 1, 1978. But our recruiting got off to a slow start, and almost all of our new employees will arrive between July 1 and December 31. So, to meet our work commitments we are achieving the necessary 25 staff years of added effort by a temporary bulge in the last few months of the year; this will cause our year-end headcount to be up 19% from January 1, and we have made our standstill projections accordingly.

As I discussed with you in May, we needed additional space to accommodate the 70 extra people, and we have rented temporary office space for them in Smallville. Since then, it has become apparent that splitting the organization would make it impossible for us to function effectively, and we have now determined that the best thing to do will be to move the entire organization to Smallville. This will actually reduce our rent bill by some 14%, which will yield a considerable long-term saving. In 1979, of course, we will incur the transitional costs of maintaining both sets of space, and we will have to pay the relocation costs for the affected employees, as well as the costs of moving equipment and office furniture. This is the chief reason why our overhead rate in 1979 will go from 142% to 257%. This other significant factor in the overhead rate rise is the large Graduate Study Program cost for the 27% of our force which is new this year (19% growth plus 8% replacement of losses). And, of course, our direct salary costs will go up by a larger percentage than those for the company overall, because most of our force has short experience and is on the steeply rising portion of the salary curves, where allotments are a large percentage of salary; we anticipate average allotments around 10.5%, compared to the company figure of 7.2%.

These factors by themselves would only increase our 1979 standstill to 182% of 1978. The rest of the increase results from unavoidable increases in paid overtime and in computer costs. We estimate that loss of effectiveness due to the extended transition to our new quarters will amount to about 25% during 1979; we will lose about another 10% due to the unusually high proportion of people in the Graduate Study Program next year. To partially offset this we plan a full working day each Saturday, which must be paid as overtime. This is a very cost-effective approach, since it increases only Direct Salary, not overhead. But it can only make up part of the gap, so we must add enough computer capacity to increase productivity by substituting computers for people. We will do this by installing computer capacity in Smallville about 50% greater than what we presently have in the region. Unfortunately, we cannot shut down our present computation facilities until the end of 1979, so our computer costs for 1979 will be about 2.5 times those of 1978, and the necessary data links between the two computation centers will increase our total rated computer center costs in 1979 to about 3.4 times the corresponding 1978 costs.

Taking these factors into account, we see that our 1979 standstill budget is approximately 228% of 1978, very close to the 229.3% shown in the detailed budget submission. I must emphasize that this does not allow for any new work; at this level we will not even be able to meet all of our existing commitments, because even with overtime and added computer capacity we cannot fully offset the temporary reduction in efficiency we will undergo in 1979.

So I must urge most strenuously that the budget not be reduced below this standstill level. Indeed, our most recent studies show that to complete our 1979 work program, including appropriate effort to reduce the backlog of deferred maintenance and enhancement work, we need to grow by 25 people in 1979, an increase of 5.7% above standstill. This would be a smaller percentage increase above standstill than we were granted in 1978, and I recommend its approval, to avoid the need for large "crisis increases" in subsequent years. May I have your concurrence to proceed on this basis?

G. Furbelow

8.2 Principles — *J. B.*

My friend was right; I had not appreciated many of the obstacles faced by large software projects. Furbelow's memo helped me to understand how software teams grow to be so big and so expensive. I now shiver with fear at the very thought of the ferocious pile of paperwork that can cover a software manager's desk.

Programmers, be kind to your poor bosses.

8.3 Further Reading

The classic reference on the management of software projects is Fred Brooks's delightful *Mythical Man Month*, published in 1975 by Addison-Wesley. The preface begins, "In many ways, managing a large computer programming project is like managing any other large undertaking—in more ways than most programmers believe." I knew Brooks was right, but I didn't realize how many "more ways" there were until I heard the problems of poor Mr. Furbelow. Fortunately, Brooks offers solutions to many management problems that arise in software projects.

Too many programmers who have spent a delightful evening with this book were so charmed by its easy reading that they failed to appreciate its wealth of factual material. If you're in that category, go back and study the book with pencil in hand.

Connoisseurs of *The Mythical Man Month* will enjoy Brooks's "No silver bullet" in the April 1987 IEEE *Computer* magazine. It is subtitled "Essence and accidents of software engineering". He defines the essential task of software engineering to be building complex conceptual constructs, while the accidental tasks involve representing the constructs in languages. The paper shows how past progress has solved many of the accidental difficulties, and surveys technologies that hold promise for solving the conceptual essence.

PART III: **I/O FIT FOR HUMANS**

Software beauty is sometimes skin deep. No matter how wonderful your program is on the inside, an ill-designed interface can drive users away. And more than one shoddy program has fooled users with snazzy input and output. Input and output may be a small part of the system from your view as a programmer, but the interface is a large part of the user's view of your software.

These columns describe several aspects of input and output. Column 9 applies principles of language design to making software interfaces that are little languages. Column 10 is about producing documents that are pleasant to look at and helpful to read. Column 11 turns to one particular part of documents: graphical displays of data. Column 12 shows how the techniques of the three previous columns were applied in computerizing a system for conducting public opinion polls.

One of the great things about making I/O fit for humans is that the exercise provides a fine excuse for talking to many interesting human beings. These columns describe how my work has brought me into contact with chemists, graphics designers, statisticians, and political scientists. This is one of the many reasons that programming is the ideal job for people like me, who can't decide what they want to be if they grow up.

Columns 9 and 10 were originally published in *Communications of the ACM* in August and September of 1986. Column 11 has been rewritten substantially since it appeared in June 1984; Sections 11.1, 11.2 and 11.6 are almost brand new. Column 12 appears for the first time in this book; parts of the text appeared in June 1984 and August 1986.

COLUMN 9: **LITTLE LANGUAGES**

When you say "language", most programmers think of the big ones, like Fortran or Cobol or Pascal. In fact, a language is any mechanism to express intent, and the input to many programs can be viewed profitably as statements in a language. This column is about those "little languages".

Programmers deal with microscopic languages every day. Consider printing a floating-point number in six characters, including a decimal point and two subsequent digits. Rather than writing a subroutine for the task, a Fortran programmer specifies the format F6.2, and a Cobol programmer defines the picture 999.99. Each of these descriptions is a statement in a well-defined little language. While the languages are quite different, each is appropriate for its problem domain. Although a Fortran programmer might complain that 999999.99999 is too long when F12.5 could do the job, the Coboler can't even express in Fortran such common financial patterns as $,$$$,$$9.99. Fortran is aimed at scientific computing, Cobol is designed for business.

In the good old days, real programmers would swagger to a key punch and, standing the whole time, crank out nine cards like:

```
//SUMMARY   JOB   REGION=(100K,50K)
//          EXEC  PGM=SUMMAR
//SYSIN     DD    DSNAME=REP.8601,DISP=OLD,
//                UNIT=2314,SPACE=(TRK,(1,1,1)),
//                VOLUME=SER=577632
//SYSOUT    DD    DSNAME=SUM.8601,DISP=(,KEEP),
//                UNIT=2314,SPACE=(TRK,(1,1,1)),
//                VOLUME=SER=577632
//SYSABEND  DD    SYSOUT=A
```

Today's young whippersnappers do this simple job by typing

```
summarize <jan.report >jan.summary
```

Modern successors to the old "job control" languages are not only more convenient to use, they are more powerful than their predecessors.

Languages surround programmers, yet many programmers don't exploit linguistic insights. Examining programs under a linguistic light can give you a better understanding of the tools you now use, and can teach you design

83

principles for building elegant interfaces to your future programs. This column will show how the user interfaces to half a dozen interesting programs can be viewed as little languages.

This column is built around Brian Kernighan's Pic language† for making line drawings. Its compiler is implemented on the UNIX system, which is particularly supportive and exploitative of language processing. (Section 12.2 shows how little languages can be implemented in a more primitive computing environment — Basic on a personal computer.)

The next section introduces Pic and the following section compares it to alternative systems. Subsequent sections discuss some little languages that compile into Pic and the little languages used to build Pic.

9.1 The Pic Language

If you're talking about compilers, you might want to depict their behavior with a picture:

(This diagram is genuine Pic output, as are all pictures in this book; we'll see its input description shortly.) Some contexts may call for a little more detail about the internal structure of the compiler. This picture shows a structure typical of many compilers:

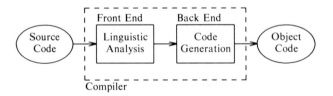

This diagram also describes the two tasks that a program for drawing pictures must perform: a back end draws the picture while a front end interprets user commands to decide what picture to draw.

And just how does a user describe a picture? There are (broadly) three ways to do the job. An interactive program allows the user to draw the program with a hand-controlled device, and a subroutine library adds picture primitives to the constructs in a programming language. We'll return to these approaches in the next section.

---

† B. W. Kernighan described "PIC — A language for typesetting graphics," in *Software — Practice and Experience 12* pp. 1–21, 1982. Kernighan describes an updated version of the language in "PIC — A graphics language for typesetting, Revised user manual", Bell Labs Computing Science Technical Report Number 116, December 1984.

The third approach to describing pictures is the topic of this column: a little language. In Kernighan's Pic language, for instance, the first figure in this section is described as

```
ellipse "Source" "Code"
arrow
box "Compiler"
arrow
ellipse "Object" "Code"
```

The first input line draws an ellipse of default size and stacks the two strings at its center. The second line draws an arrow in the default direction (moving right), and the third line draws a box with the text at its center. The implicit motion after each object makes it easy to draw the picture and convenient to add new objects to an existing picture.

This nonsense picture illustrates several other devices that Pic supports, including lines, double arrowheads, and dashed boxes.

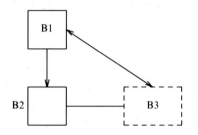

The program that draws it places objects by implicit motions, by explicit motions, and by connecting existing objects:

```
boxht = .4; boxwid = .4
down      # set default direction
B1: box "B1"
arrow
B2: box
"B2 " at B2.w rjust
line right .6 from B2.e
B3: box dashed wid .6 "B3"
line <-> from B3.n to B1.e
```

The boxht and boxwid variables represent the default height and width of a box in inches. Those values can also be explicitly set in the definition of a particular box. Text following the # character is a comment, up to the end of the line. Labels such as B1, B2 and B3 name objects; LongerName is fine too. The western point of box B2 is referred to as B2.w; one could also refer to B2.n or B2.nw, for the northwest corner. A line of the form *string* at *position* places a text string at a given position; rjust right-justifies the string (strings can also be left justified or placed above or below positions).

These devices were used to draw this figure, which gives a yet more detailed view of a compiler.

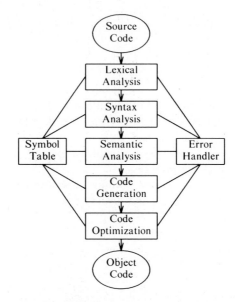

Any particular compiler translates one source language into one object language. How can an organization maintain 5 different languages on 5 different machines? A brute-force approach writes 25 compilers:

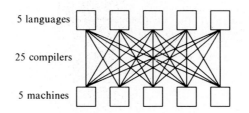

An *intermediate language* circumvents much of this complexity. A new language is installed by writing a front end that translates into the intermediate language, and a new machine is installed by a back end that translates the intermediate language into the machine's output code:

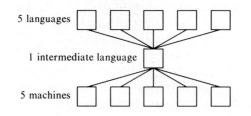

If there are *L* languages on *M* machines, the brute-force approach constructs *L*×*M* distinct compilers, while the intermediate language needs just *L* front ends and *M* back ends. (Pic compiles its output into a picture-drawing subset of the Troff typesetting language, which in turn produces an intermediate language suitable for interpretation on a number of output devices, from terminal display programs to laser printers to phototypesetters.)

The last figure uses two Pic programming constructs, variables and loops:

```
n = 5                                # number of langs & machines
boxht = boxwid = .2
h = .3; w = .35                      # height & width for spacing
I: box at w*(n+1)/2,0                # intermediate language box
for i = 1 to n do {
    box with .s at i*w, h            # language box
    line from last box.s to I.n
    box with .n at i*w, -h           # machine box
    line from last box.n to I.s
}
"1 intermediate language  " at I.w rjust
"5 languages  " at 2nd box .w rjust
"5 machines  " at 3rd box .w rjust
```

The picture of the brute-force approach is described by a single loop to draw the boxes, followed by two nested loops to make all pairwise interconnections.

The examples in this section should give you an idea of the structure of Pic, but they only hint at its power. I have not mentioned a number of Pic's facilities, such as built-in functions, if statements, macro processing, file inclusion, and a simple block structure.

9.2 Perspective

In this section we'll consider several approaches to picture-drawing programs and compare them to Pic. Although the particulars are for pictures, the general lessons apply to designing user interfaces for many kinds of programs.

An interactive drawing program allows the user to enter a picture with a spatial input device such as a mouse or a drawing pad and displays the picture as it is drawn. Most interactive systems have a menu that includes items such as boxes, ellipses, and lines of various flavors (vertical, horizontal, dotted, etc.). Immediate feedback makes such systems quite comfortable for drawing many simple pictures, but drawing this picture on an interactive system would require a steady hand and the patience of Job:

Pic's programming constructs allow the picture to be drawn easily:

```
pi = 3.14159; n = 10; r = .4
s = 2*pi/n
for i = 1 to n-1 do {
    for j = i+1 to n do {
        line from r*cos(s*i), r*sin(s*i)\
             to    r*cos(s*j), r*sin(s*j)
    }
}
```

(The backslash character \ at the end of a line allows the line to be continued on the next line.)

But handy as such features are, doesn't parsimony† dictate that variables and for loops properly belong in a full programming language? This concern is addressed by a subroutine library that adds pictures to the primitives supported by a given language. Given a subroutine line(x1, y1, x2, y2), one could easily draw the last picture in Pascal:

```
pi := 3.14159; n := 10; r := 0.4;
s := 2*pi/n;
for i := 1 to n-1 do
    for j := i+1 to n do
        line (r*cos(s*i), r*sin(s*i),
              r*cos(s*j), r*sin(s*j) );
```

Unfortunately, to draw this picture

one must write, compile, execute, and debug a program containing subroutine calls like these:

```
ellipse(0.3, 0, 0.6, 0.4)
text(0.3, 0, "Input")
arrow(0.75, 0, 0.3, 0)
box(1.2, 0, 0.6, 0.4)
text(1.2, 0, "Processor")
arrow(1.65, 0, 0.3, 0)
ellipse(2.1, 0, 0.6, 0.4)
text(2.1, 0, "Output")
```

Even such simple code may be too hard for some nonprogrammers who find Pic

---

† Arguments beyond taste suggest that Pic's for loops may be inappropriate: their syntax differs from similar loops elsewhere in the UNIX system, and Pic's for loops are orders of magnitude slower than those in other languages. Purists may write loops in other languages to generate Pic output; I am a delighted if compromised user of Pic's for loops — the quilts and stereograms in the exercises were easy to generate using that construct.

comfortable, such as technical typists or software managers. The first two arguments to each routine give the x and y coordinates of the center of the object; later arguments give its width and height or a text string. These routines are rather primitive; more clever routines might, for instance, have an implicit motion associated with objects.

So far I've used the term "little language" intuitively. The time has come for a more precise definition. I'll restrict the term computer language to textual inputs, and thus ignore the spatial and temporal languages defined by cursor movements and button clicks.

> A computer language enables a textual description of an object to be processed by a computer program.

The object being described might vary widely, from a picture to a program to a tax form. Defining "little" is harder: it might imply that a first-time user can use the system in half an hour or master the language in a day, or perhaps that the first implementation took just a few days. In any case, a little language is specialized to a particular problem domain and does not include many features found in conventional languages.

Pic qualifies in my book as a little language, although admittedly a big little language. Its tutorial and user manual is 26 pages long (including over 50 sample pictures); I built my first picture in well under an hour. Kernighan had the first implementation up and stumbling within a week of putting pencil to coding form. The current version is about 4000 lines of C code and represents several months of effort spread over five years. Although Pic has many features of big languages (variables, for statements, and labels), it is missing many other features (declarations, while and case statements, and facilities for separate compilation). I won't attempt a more precise definition of a little language; if the linguistic analogy gives you insight into a particular program, use it, and if it doesn't, ignore it.

We have considered three different approaches to specifying pictures: interactive systems, subroutine libraries, and little languages. Which one is best? Well, that depends.

> Interactive systems are probably the easiest to use for drawing simple pictures, but a large collection of pictures may be hard to manage. (Given 50 pictures in a long paper, how do you make all ellipses 0.1 inches wider and 0.05 inches shorter?)

> If your pictures are generated by big programs, subroutine libraries can be easy and efficient. Libraries are usually uncomfortable for drawing simple pictures, though.

> Little languages are a natural way to describe many pictures; they can be integrated easily into document production systems to include pictures in larger documents. Pictures can be managed using familiar tools such as file systems and text editors.

I've used picture-drawing programs based on each of the three models: interactive drawers, subroutine libraries, and little languages. Each type of system is handy for drawing some pictures and awkward for others.†

9.3 Pic Preprocessors

One of the greatest advantages of little languages is that one processor's input can be another processor's output. So far we've only thought of Pic as an input language. In this section we'll briefly survey two very small languages for describing specialized classes of pictures; their compilers generate Pic programs as output.

We'll start with Scatter, a Pic preprocessor that makes scatter plots from x,y data. The output of Scatter is fed as input to Pic, which in turn feeds the Troff document formatter.

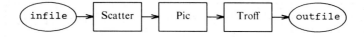

This structure is easy to implement as a UNIX pipeline of processes:

```
scatter infile ¦ pic ¦ troff >outfile
```

(The UNIX Shell that interprets such commands is, of course, another little language. In addition to the ¦ operator for constructing pipelines, the language includes common programming commands such as if, case, for and while.)

Pic is a big little language, Scatter is at the other end of the spectrum. This Scatter input uses all five kinds of commands in the language.

```
size x 1.8
size y 1.2
range x 1870 1990
range y 35 240
label x Year
label y Population
ticks x 1880 1930 1980
ticks y 50 100 150 200
file pop.d
```

The size commands give the width (x) and height (y) of the frame in inches. The range commands tell the spread of the dimensions, and labels and ticks

---

† In terms of implementation difficulty, all three approaches have a front end for specification and a back end for picture drawing. Subroutine libraries use a language's procedure mechanism as a front end: it may be clumsy, but it's familiar and free. Little languages can use standard compiler technology for their front end; we'll see such tools in Section 9.4. Because interactive systems usually involve real-time graphics, they are typically the hardest to implement and the least portable (often with two back ends: an interactive one shows the picture as it is being drawn, and a static one writes the complete picture to a file).

are similarly specified. Ranges are mandatory for both dimensions; all other specifications are optional. The description must also specify an input file containing x,y pairs. The first few lines in the file pop.d are

```
1880      50.19
1890      62.98
1900      76.21
1910      92.22
1920      106.02
```

The x-value is a year and the y-value is the United States population in millions in the census of that year. Scatter turns that simple description of a scatter plot into a 23-line Pic program that produces this graph:

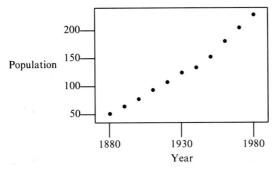

The Scatter language is tiny but useful. Its "compiler" is a 24-line Awk program that I built in just under an hour. (In many environments, Snobol's string-processing facilities would make it the language of choice for quickly implementing a little language; Awk is a more natural choice in my UNIX environment.) A slightly larger little language for drawing graphs is described in Section 6.2 of *The AWK Programming Language* (cited in Section 2.6); it is not a Pic preprocessor, but rather prints the graph as an array of characters.

Chemists often draw chemical structure diagrams like this representation of the antibiotic penicillin G:

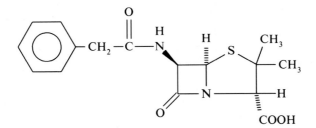

A chemist could draw that picture in Pic, but it is a tedious and time-consuming task. It is more natural for an author with a chemical background to describe

the structure in the Chem language, using familiar terms like benzene rings, double bonds, and back bonds:

```
R1: ring4 pointing 45 put N at 2
    doublebond -135 from R1.V3 ; O
    backbond up from R1.V1 ; H
    frontbond -45 from R1.V4 ; N
    H above N
    bond left from N ; C
    doublebond up ; O
    bond length .1 left from C ; CH2
    bond length .1 left
    benzene pointing left
R2: flatring5 put S at 1 put N at 4 with .V5 at R1.V1
    bond 20 from R2.V2 ; CH3
    bond 90 from R2.V2 ; CH3
    bond 90 from R2.V3 ; H
    backbond 170 from R2.V3 ; COOH
```

The history of Chem is typical of many little languages. Late one Monday afternoon, Brian Kernighan and I spent an hour with Lynn Jelinski, a Bell Labs chemist, moaning about the difficulty of writing. She described the hassles of including chemical structures in her documents: the high cost and inordinate delays of dealing with a drafting department. We suspected that her task might be appropriate for a Pic preprocessor, so she lent us a recent monograph rich in chemical diagrams.

That evening Kernighan and I each designed a microscopic language that could describe many of the structures, and implemented them with Awk processors, each about 50 lines long. Our model of the world was way off base — the book was about polymers, so our languages were biased towards linear structures. Nevertheless, the output was impressive enough to convince Jelinski to spend a couple of hours educating us about the real problem. By Wednesday we had built a set of Pic macros with which Jelinski could, with some pain, draw structures of genuine interest to her; that convinced her to spend even more time on the project. Over the next few days we built and threw away several little languages that compiled into those macros. A week after starting the project, the three of us had designed and implemented the rudiments of the current Chem language, whose evolution since then has been guided by real users. The current version is about 500 lines of Awk and uses a library of about 70 lines of Pic macros. Jelinski, Kernighan, and I describe the language and present the complete code in *Computers and Chemistry*, vol. 11, no. 4, pp. 281–297, 1987.

These two brief examples hint at the power of preprocessors for little languages. Pic produces line drawings. Scatter extends it to scatter plots and Chem deals with chemical structures. Each preprocessor was easy to implement by compiling into Pic. It would be more difficult to extend interactive drawing programs to new problem domains such as graphs or chemistry.

9.4 Little Languages for Implementing Pic

In this section we'll turn from using Pic to building it. We'll study three UNIX tools that Kernighan used to construct the Pic language. Each of the tools can be viewed as providing a little language for describing part of the programmer's job. This section briefly sketches the three tools; the Further Reading describes all of them in detail. The purpose of this section is to hint at the breadth of little languages; you may skip to the next section any time you feel overwhelmed by the details.

An earlier figure illustrates the components in a typical compiler; this figure shows that Pic has many, but not all, of those components:

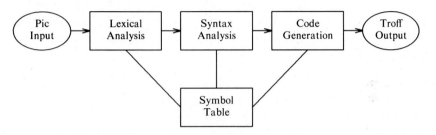

We'll first study the Lex program, which generates Pic's lexical analyzer. Then we'll turn to Yacc, which performs the syntax analysis. Finally we'll look at Make, which manages the 40 source, object, header, testing and documentation files used by Pic.

A lexical analyzer (or lexer) breaks the input text into units called tokens. It is usually implemented as a subroutine; at each call it returns the next token in the input text. For instance, on the Pic input line

```
L: line dashed down .8 left .4 from B1.s
```

a lexer should return the following sequence:

```
SYMBOL: L
LINE
DASHED
DOWN
NUMBER: 0.8
LEFT
NUMBER: 0.4
FROM
SYMBOL: B1
SOUTH
```

Constructing a lexer is straightforward but tedious, and therefore ideal work for a computer. Mike Lesk's Lex language specifies a lexer by a series of pattern-action pairs. The Lex program reads that description and builds a C routine to implement the lexer. When the lexer recognizes the regular expression on the left, it performs the action on the right. Here is a fragment of the Lex description of Pic:

```
">"                     return(GT);
"<"                     return(LT);
">="                    return(GE);
"<="                    return(LE);
"<-"                    return(HEAD1);
"->"                    return(HEAD2);
"<->"                   return(HEAD12);
"."(s|south)            return(SOUTH);
"."(b|bot|bottom)       return(SOUTH);
```

The regular expression (a|b) denotes either a or b. Given a description in this form, the Lex program generates a C function that performs lexical analysis.

Those regular expressions are simple; Pic's definition of a floating point number is more interesting:

```
({D}+("."?){D}*|"."{D}+)((e|E)("+"|-)?{D}+)
```

The string "{D}" denotes the digits 0..9. (In the spirit of this column, observe that regular expressions are a microscopic language for describing patterns in text strings.) Constructing a recognizer for that monster is tedious and error-prone work for a human. Lex quickly and accurately constructs a lexer from a description that is easy to prepare.

Yacc is an acronym for "Yet Another Compiler-Compiler". Steve Johnson's program is a parser generator; it can be viewed as a little language for describing languages. Its input has roughly the same pattern-action form as Awk and Lex: when a pattern on the left-hand side is recognized, the action on the right is performed. While Lex's patterns are regular expressions, Yacc supports context-free languages. Here is part of Pic's definition of an arithmetic expression:

```
expr:
    NUMBER
  | VARNAME        { $$ = getfval($1); }
  | expr '+' expr  { $$ = $1 + $3; }
  | expr '-' expr  { $$ = $1 - $3; }
  | expr '*' expr  { $$ = $1 * $3; }
  | expr '/' expr  { if ($3 == 0.0) {
                         error("division by zero");
                         $3 = 1.0;
                     }
                     $$ = $1 / $3; }
  | '(' expr ')'   { $$ = $2; }
    ...
  ;
```

Given a description like this, Yacc builds a parser. When the parser finds expr + expr, it returns (in $$) the sum of the first expression ($1) and the second

expression (which is the third object, $3). The complete definition describes the
precedence of operators (* binds before +), comparison operators (such as <
and >), functions, and several other minor complications.

A Pic program can be viewed as a sequence of primitive geometric objects.
A primitive is defined as

```
primitive:
    BOX attrlist        { boxgen($1); }
  | CIRCLE attrlist     { elgen($1); }
  | ELLIPSE attrlist    { elgen($1); }
  | ARC attrlist        { arcgen($1); }
  | LINE attrlist       { linegen($1); }
    ...
  ;
```

When the parser sees an `ellipse` statement, it parses the attribute list and
then calls the routine `elgen`. It passes to that routine the first component in
the phrase, the token `ELLIPSE`. The `elgen` routine uses that token to decide
whether to generate a general ellipse or a circle (a special-case ellipse with
length equal to width).

All Pic primitives have the same attribute list; some primitives, however,
ignore some attributes. An attribute list is either empty or an attribute list followed by an attribute:

```
attrlist:
    attrlist attr
  | /* empty */
  ;
```

And here is a small part of the definition of an attribute:

```
attr:
    DIR expr        { storefattr($1, !DEF, $2); }
  | DIR             { storefattr($1, DEF, 0.0); }
  | FROM position   { storeoattr($1, $2); }
  | TO position     { storeoattr($1, $2); }
  | AT position     { storeoattr($1, $2); }
    ...
  ;
```

As each attribute is parsed, the appropriate routine stores its value. This is an
elegant implementation of the name-value pairs discussed in Section 4.1.

These tools tackle well-studied problems. The compiler book cited in Section
9.7 devotes 80 pages to lexers and 120 pages to parsers. Lex and Yacc package
that technology: the programmer defines the lexical and syntactic structure in
straightforward little languages, and the programs generate high-quality processors. Not only are the descriptions easy to generate in the first place, they make
the language easy to modify.

Stu Feldman's Make program addresses a more mundane problem that is
nonetheless difficult and crucial for large programs: keeping up-to-date versions

of the files containing header code, source code, object code, documentation, test cases, etc. Here is an abbreviated version of the file that Kernighan uses to describe the files associated with Pic:

```
OFILES = picy.o picl.o main.o print.o \
         misc.o symtab.o blockgen.o \
         ...
CFILES = main.c print.c misc.c symtab.c \
         blockgen.c boxgen.c circgen.c \
         ...
SRCFILES = picy.y picl.l pic.h $(CFILES)
pic:    $(OFILES)
        cc $(OFILES) -lm
$(OFILES): pic.h y.tab.h
manual:
        pic manual | eqn | troff -ms >manual.out
backup: $(SRCFILES) makefile pictest.a manual
        push safemachine $? /usr/bwk/pic
        touch backup
bundle:
        bundle $(SRCFILES) makefile README
```

The file starts with the definition of three names: OFILES are the object files, CFILES contain C code, and the source files SRCFILES consist of the C files and the Yacc description picy.y, the Lex description picl.l, and a header file. The next line states that Pic must have up-to-date versions of object files (Make's internal tables tell how to make object files from source files). The next line tells how to combine those into a current version of Pic. The following line states that the object files depend on the two named header files. When Kernighan types make pic, Make checks the currency of all object files (file.o is current if its modification time is later than file.c), recompiles out-of-date modules, then loads the needed pieces along with the appropriate function libraries.

The next two lines tell what happens when Kernighan types make manual: the file containing the user manual is processed by Troff and two preprocessors. The backup command saves on safemachine all modified files, and the bundle command wraps the named files into a package suitable for mailing. Although Make was originally designed specifically with compiling in mind, Feldman's elegant general mechanism gracefully supports all these additional housekeeping functions.

9.5 Principles

Little languages are an important part of the popular Fourth- and Fifth-Generation Languages and Application Generators, but their influence on computing is broader. Little languages often provide an elegant interface for humans to control complex programs or for modules in a large system to communicate with one another. Although most of the examples in this column are large "systems programs" on the UNIX system, Section 12.2 shows how the ideas were used in a fairly mundane data processing system implemented in Basic on a microcomputer.

The principles of language design summarized below are well known among designers of big programming languages. They are just as relevant to the design of little languages.

Design Goals. Before you design a language, carefully study the problem you are trying to solve. Should you instead build a subroutine library or an interactive system? An old rule of thumb states that the first 10 percent of programming effort provides 90 percent of the functionality; can you make do with an Awk or Basic or Snobol implementation that cheaply provides the first 90 percent, or do you have to use more powerful tools like Lex and Yacc and Make to get to 99.9 percent?

Simplicity. Keep your language as simple as possible. A smaller language is easier for its implementers to design, build, document and maintain and is easier for its users to learn and use.

Fundamental Abstractions. Typical computer languages are built around the world-view of a von Neumann computer: instructions operate on small chunks of data. The designer of a little language has to be more creative: the primitive objects might be geometric symbols, chemical structures, context-free languages, or the files in a program. Operations on objects vary just as widely, from fusing two benzene rings to recompiling a source file. Identifying these key players is old hat to programmers; the primitive objects are a program's abstract data types, and the operations are the key subroutines.

Linguistic Structure. Once you know the basic objects and operations, there are still many ways of writing down their interactions. The infix arithmetic expression 2+3*4 might be written in postfix as 234*+ or functionally as plus(2,times(3,4)); there is often a tradeoff between naturalness of expression and ease of implementation. But whatever else you may or may not include in your language, be sure to allow indentation and comments.

Yardsticks of Language Design. Rather than preach about tasteful design, I've chosen as examples useful languages that illustrate good taste. Here are some of their desirable properties.

Orthogonality: keep unrelated features unrelated.

Generality: use an operation for many purposes.

Parsimony: delete unneeded operations.

Completeness: can the language describe all objects of interest?

Similarity: make the language as suggestive as possible.

Extensibility: make sure the language can grow.

Openness: let the user "escape" to use related tools.

The Design Process. Like other great software, great little languages are grown, not built. Start with a solid, simple design, expressed in a notation like Backus-Naur form. Before implementing the language, test your design by describing a wide variety of objects in the proposed language. After the language is up and running, iterate designs to add features as dictated by the needs of your customers.

Insights from Compiler Building. When you build the processor for your little language, don't forget lessons from compilers. As much as possible, separate the linguistic analysis in the front end from the processing in the back end; that will make the processor easier to build and easier to port to a new system or new use of the language. And when you need them, use compiler-building tools like Lex, Yacc and Make.

9.6 Problems

1. Most systems provide a package for sorting files; the interface is usually a little language. Evaluate the language provided by your system. The UNIX system sort, for instance, is invoked by a command like

   ```
   sort -t: +3n
   ```

   This line says to use the character : as the field separator and to sort the file so that the fourth field (skip the first three fields) occurs in numeric order. Design a less cryptic language and implement it, perhaps as a preprocessor that generates commands for your system sort.

2. Lex uses a little language for regular expressions to specify lexical analyzers. What other programs on your system employ regular expressions? How do they differ, and why?

3. Study different languages for describing bibliographic references. How do the languages differ in applications such as document retrieval systems and bibliography programs in document production systems? How are little languages used to perform queries in each system?

4. Study examples of what might be the littlest languages of them all: assemblers, format descriptions, and stack languages.

5. Many people can perceive a three-dimensional image by crossing their eyes and fusing the two halves of stereograms:

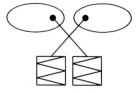

A small survey I conducted suggests that about half the readers of this column should be able to perceive these three-dimensional scenes; the other half will get a headache trying.

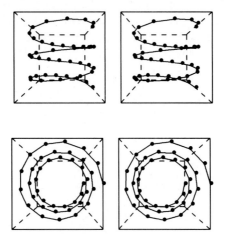

These pictures were drawn by a 40-line Pic program. Design and implement a three-dimensional language for describing stereograms.

6. Design and implement little languages. Interesting pictorial domains include electrical diagrams, data structures such as arrays, trees, and graphs (drawing Finite State Machines like those in Section 2.2 is especially interesting) and pictorially scored games, such as bowling and baseball. Another interesting domain is describing musical scores. Consider both rendering the score on a sheet of paper and playing it on a music generator.

7. Design a little language to deal with common forms in your organization, such as expense reports for trips.

8. How can processors of little languages respond to linguistic errors? (Consider the options available to compilers for large languages.) How do particular processors respond to errors?

9.7 Further Reading

You may never have heard of *Compilers: Principles, Techniques, and Tools* by Aho, Sethi and Ullman, but you'd probably recognize the cover of the "New Dragon Book" (published in 1986 by Addison-Wesley). And you *can* judge this book by its cover: it is an excellent introduction to the field of compilers, with a healthy emphasis on little languages. Furthermore, the book makes extensive use of Pic to tell its story in pictures. (Most of the compiler pictures in this column were inspired by pictures in that book.)

Chapter 8 of *The UNIX Programming Environment* by Kernighan and Pike (Prentice-Hall, 1984) is the case history of a little language. They start with a language for evaluating expressions, then add variables and functions, and finally add control constructs and user-defined functions to achieve a fairly expressive programming language. Throughout the process Kernighan and Pike use the UNIX tools sketched in this column to design, develop and document their language. Chapter 6 of *The AWK Programming Language* cited in Section 2.6 describes how Awk can easily process very little languages.

COLUMN 10: **DOCUMENT DESIGN**

FOR A LONG TIME, COMPUTER OUTPUT LOOKED LIKE THIS. As time went on, printers acquired lower case letters and special characters!@#&%?! Then slow little daisy wheel printers started producing output so fine that it was called "typewriter-quality". The printers offered new characters, such as *italic* fonts, and other typographic niceties, such as subscripting.

Mechanical printers store letter images in pieces of metal; laser printers store letterforms as bits. (At last, something we programmers can get our hands on!) Laser printers therefore typically come with a wide variety of fonts, *some* more exotic than **others**, and the ability to make text larger or smaller.

The first laser printers were expensive and huge, but technological advances have since reduced their cost to a few thousand dollars and a couple of square feet on a desk. Document production systems, such as Scribe, TEX and Troff, place the capabilities of the devices comfortably within the grasp of programmers. Personal computers have spread the technology even more widely. The popular press touts the revolution in "desktop publishing". Because they are the resident experts for all computing tools, many programmers have recently turned into amateur typesetters, with tools superior to those used by professionals just a decade ago.

And that brings good news and bad. The good news is obvious: we programmers can use these powerful tools to construct documents that are handsome to look at and easy to read. Many programmers now routinely typeset program documentation, course notes, technical reports, and articles for conference proceedings. The bad news, unfortunately, is sometimes even more obvious: most programmers haven't thought much about document design, and ☞powerful tools can sometimes be *powerfully* ABUSED◀!!!

Like most programmers, I have no training in book design. I first wrote this column shortly after I typeset my 1986 book *Programming Pearls*. During that project, I learned a great deal from professional book designers at Addison-Wesley and from several Bell Labs colleagues who were writing and typesetting books at that time. This column is my attempt to pass on some of the more important lessons I learned during that exercise.

101

The previous column discussed several little languages for controlling typographical programs. This column turns from the mechanism of document production to the appearance of the documents that we produce. The column is
aimed at programmers who design and typeset their own documents. Programmers not involved in typesetting may also enjoy parts of this column: documents
employ general design principles that are also relevant to software.

The next section is a detailed discussion of one diminutive domain: typesetting tables. The following section presents three design principles underlying
tables and other typography. The two subsequent sections treat figures and
text, and the final section considers the issue of selecting the right medium to
present an idea.

10.1 Tables

One could describe the sizes and populations of the various continents with a
series of sentences, starting with "Asia comprises 16,999,000 square miles,
which is 29.7% of the land area of the earth; its population is 2,897,000,000, or
59.8% of the world's population." That information is communicated more
effectively by this table, which is easy to generate on many document production systems. This table, like all other tables in this book, was produced by
Mike Lesk's Tbl program. (Tbl is a little language for describing tables; it is
implemented as yet another preprocessor for Troff.)

Continent	Area	%Earth	Pop.	%Total
Asia	16,999,000	29.7	2,897,000,000	59.8
Africa	11,688,000	20.4	551,000,000	11.4
North America	9,366,000	16.3	400,000,000	8.3
South America	6,881,000	12.0	271,000,000	5.6
Antarctica	5,100,000	8.9	0	0
Europe	4,017,000	7.0	702,000,000	14.5
Australia	2,966,000	5.2	16,000,000	0.3

The remainder of this section is an exercise in table design. We'll hold constant the numbers and continent names that are the body of the table, and alter
other design parameters in three additional tables. The next version of the table
uses a Helvetica font,† provides more descriptive titles, centers the table within
the margins, centers the continent names, and adds vertical and horizontal lines

---

† The house style of *Communications of the ACM* in which this column originally appeared dictates
that all tables shall be in a Helvetica font. One of the reasons is that tables are set in a small (8-
point) text size, and small text is a little easier to read in Helvetica.

(called rules). Because the numbers are expressed in more natural units, the
next table is narrow enough to fit in a single column of *Communications of the
ACM* (the first table had to span two columns when this column first appeared
in that publication; just as in programming, typographical space is often free
but sometimes costs dearly).

Continent	Area		Population	
	Mill. Sq. Mi.	%	Mill.	%
Asia	16.999	29.7	2,897	59.8
Africa	11.688	20.4	551	11.4
North America	9.366	16.3	400	8.3
South America	6.881	12.0	271	5.6
Antarctica	5.100	8.9	0	0
Europe	4.017	7.0	702	14.5
Australia	2.966	5.2	16	0.3

Rules are helpful in guiding the reader's eye, but the above table has too
much of a good thing. The next table makes do with fewer rules, and doubles
some of the more important ones to reflect their importance in the data set.
Centering the names is also overdone, so we'll change them back to left-
justified. We'll use a smaller typeface (9 points instead of 10), and we'll shrink
the vertical spacing from 12 points to 11 points. The headings are reworded (as
they are in each table in this series), and they are emphasized with a bold font.

Continent	Area		Population	
	10^6 Sq. Mi.	% of Total	Millions	% of Total
Asia	16.999	29.7	2,897	59.8
Africa	11.688	20.4	551	11.4
North America	9.366	16.3	400	8.3
South America	6.881	12.0	271	5.6
Antarctica	5.100	8.9	0	0
Europe	4.017	7.0	702	14.5
Australia	2.966	5.2	16	0.3

The next version of the table is my personal favorite. It is inspired by the
guidelines in Chapter 12 of *The Chicago Manual of Style* cited in Section 10.8.
It uses as few rules as possible. The only double rule is on top, to set the table
off from the preceding text. I'd like to distinguish the headings from the text,
but the bold font in the previous table is too violent. The next table therefore
uses SMALL CAPITALS for the major headings and leaves the others alone. For

similar reasons, the primary font is changed from Helvetica back to the original Times Roman.

CONTINENT	LAND AREA		POPULATION	
	Millions of Square Miles	Percent	Millions	Percent
Asia	16.999	29.7	2,897	59.8
Africa	11.688	20.4	551	11.4
North America	9.366	16.3	400	8.3
South America	6.881	12.0	271	5.6
Antarctica	5.100	8.9	0	0
Europe	4.017	7.0	702	14.5
Australia	2.966	5.2	16	0.3

Although the four tables in this section contain the same data, their appearances are quite different. The best table design for a given document depends on a number of factors, ranging from the capabilities of the document production system (what can it do easily or at all?) to the purpose of the document (advertising should reach out and grab the reader's eye, while a manual should provide easy reference).

This discussion of the superficial appearance of tables has neglected many fundamental issues in table design. The general form of all four tables is acceptable; it could have been worse (by swapping the rows and columns, for instance, or by re-ordering some rows or columns). Laying out tables with more elaborate structure can be challenging. All the tables, though, fail miserably in the description of the data: What is the source? How and when were the numbers gathered? Good tables tell who, what, where, when, why and how. This discussion entirely ignored the most important aspect of the table: What do the numbers mean? What do we do with them? As important as these issues are, though, they transcend the typographical theme of this column.

10.2 Three Design Principles

But wait just a minute! This column is for programmers, and we all know how real programmers feel about documentation of any kind: slap it together as quickly as possible so you can get back to the fun of programming. I won't try to convince hard-core code junkies that documentation is important, but I think that even they might have something to learn from document design.

Everyone should read Strunk and White's classic little *Elements of Style*; the third edition was published by Macmillan in 1979. What Strunk and White do for English text, Kernighan and Plauger do for programs in their *Elements of Programming Style* (second edition, McGraw-Hill, 1978). Some of the principles they enunciate also apply to document design. Here are three fundamental principles for producing better text, programs, or documents.

Iteration. Strunk and White advise authors to "Revise and rewrite." Good programmers have long known this; Kernighan and Plauger's *Elements of*

Programming Style is built around the revision of programs from textbooks. It took a lot of work to get from the first table to the last version, but an attractive document is sometimes worth the effort.

Consistency. One could spend a lifetime revising and rewriting a single document. Strunk and White avoid this problem by counselling us to "Choose a suitable design and hold to it." Some programmers have their design dictated by a shop-wide coding standard. A good standard is a delight, and a poor standard is often better than none at all. Experiment to find the best style for a particular kind of document, then stick to it.

Minimalism. Because "vigorous writing is concise," Strunk and White tell us to "Omit needless words." Robust, efficient and maintainable programs are also concise; good programmers omit needless lines, variables and routines. I once heard a programmer praised with "He adds function by deleting code." Try to remove as much as possible from your documents, such as *superfluous* font **changes** and <u>excess rules</u>, without reducing the information content.

10.3 Figures

Let's apply those principles to typesetting figures. We'll start with binary search in a sorted array, which is described in Section 3.1. Figure 1 shows a binary search for 50 in an array of 16 elements: the first probe compares 50 to the middle (eighth) element of the array (41), the second probe looks at the twelfth element, and so forth, until the fourth probe finds 50 in the eleventh position. The size, positioning, font and legend of Figure 1 are typical of many pictures produced on personal computers.

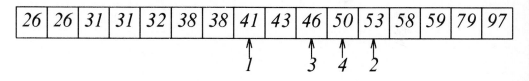

Figure 1. **Binary search** in an array.

A few experiments gave the next version of the figure, which uses more delicate lines and shrinks the boxes and text to fit comfortably within the margins. It also varies the length of the arrows that represent the probes, so the arrows get shorter as the probes get nearer the target.

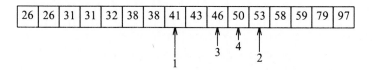

Removing the ugly figure caption saves space and placing the figure within the paragraph saves the reader the effort of scanning for a figure number.

Page 391 of the May 1986 *Communications of the ACM* describes a system for typesetting music with a figure in an area of about 6×6.5 inches:

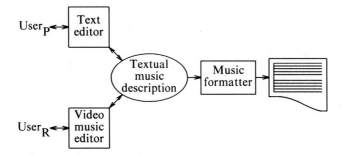

By shrinking a few pieces of geometry and rotating the diagram to flow across the page rather than down it, this figure does the same job in about one tenth of the area of the original (and space in that magazine does matter dearly). Shrinking figures not only saves space, but the final product looks more professional than its larger cousins. Try it.

The next column discusses a class of figure used commonly in technical writing: graphs. This graph, for instance, shows a path through a direction field that is the solution to a differential equation.

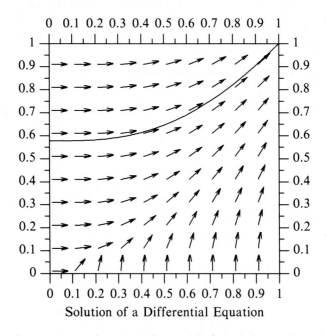

Solution of a Differential Equation

The next version presents the same data with fewer distractions. It has more informative labels, fewer ticks (the four in this version tell as much as the 84 in the original), and reduced size. The garish arrows have been replaced by more subtle lines.

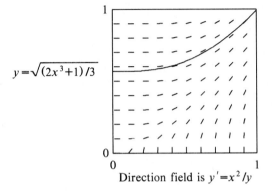

$$y=\sqrt{(2x^3+1)/3}$$

Direction field is $y'=x^2/y$

Many picture programs offer elaborate shading patterns that are frequently eye-catching and sometimes insightful. Too often, though, they obscure the message and induce vertigo. Some systems produce color figures, which can be incredibly powerful (if you disagree, try reading a black-and-white xerographic copy of a color road map). But color is almost always expensive to reproduce, and is often overused. Be careful with these devices.

The width of lines in a drawing can change the character of a figure. Here is a flow graph rendered in three different line widths:

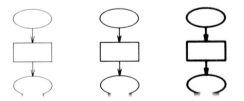

Thin lines fade away, while thick lines look heavy-handed. Strive for balance.

The previous section sketched three design principles: iteration, consistency, and minimalism. The before-and-after pictures in this section show that iteration is just as relevant for pictures as for any other design. Here are a few minimalistic points that I try to use consistently in figures.

Keep figures small, but big enough to read comfortably.

Keep figures near the text they amplify. When possible, integrate figures into the text and do away with captions and figure numbers.

Use color and background shadings sparingly.

Use delicate line widths.

10.4 Text

Tables and figures provide fine seasoning now and then, but the meat and potatoes of any document is text: paragraphs made of sentences made of words. Here are a few points about producing text that are often neglected in documents written by programmers.

Font and Size Changes. You know the topic of this paragraph because the first four words are in an italic font. That font is quite helpful for noting the *definition* of a technical term and for displaying mathematical variables (like x, y and z). Changing the size of text is also sometimes useful.† Beware the temptation to overuse these devices: a page full of font and size changes is hard for the eye to traverse.

Display Lists. Text doesn't always come wrapped neatly in paragraphs; there are many other ways to deliver words.

1. To make a sequence of similar points, try a sequence of indented paragraphs.

2. This mechanism draws the reader's attention to the similarities and the differences in the points.

3. Don't overdecorate. The numbers in this example are useless. They could be replaced by bullets or, better yet, nothing.

This display list is abused; a paragraph would have served just as well. The display list at the end of the previous section is more appropriate.

White Space. Use space to set apart the components of a document: paragraphs, elements in a display list, figures, or tables. Just as silence is important in telling a story aloud, space is crucial in laying out a document. Too little space is likeastorywithoutanypauses, while too much space, uhh, is, well, just as, ummmm, you know, unbearable.

Page Format. This is the first thing a reader observes in your document. The chapter and section titles should provide a visual outline of the document but not be so overwhelming that they chop it into incoherent pieces. The same holds for captions of tables, figures, programs and the like. The running heads should inform yet not clutter.

Page Layout. Once you have the content and the page format, the final step is to put the product into the package. Try to keep a table or a figure near the text that describes it; if you can't put the figure on the same page, try for the opposite page rather than the back of the page. Other niceties include page balancing to ensure that opposing pages are the same length and removing widows and orphans (a single word on the last line in a paragraph or a single line at the top of a page) and rivers (streams of space running vertically through text).

---

† Footnotes are small yet still readable. Their parenthetical nature is reflected in a reduced page budget. Smaller text is also often used in long quotations, exercises, solutions, bibliographies, and other supporting text.

The Publication Process. Before a paper appears on the pages of a typical journal, it receives the attention of many people. The author's technical contribution is examined and often improved by a technical editor and referees. A house editor then marks the writing style to conform to house style, and a printer sets type to prepare galley proofs. A professional artist simultaneously prepares figures. After an editor proofreads the pieces, they are laid out to form the page proofs. A lone programmer lacks the experience and taste of this gang of trained professionals, but has the advantage of being able to consider a problem from many viewpoints (if a figure doesn't fit on a page, a programmer might float the figure to the next page, shrink it a little, rewrite surrounding text, or so on). Use your flexibility to advantage, but carefully consider any advice you can get from the professionals.

The Logical Structure of Text. After this column appeared in *Communications of the ACM*, Leslie Lamport of Digital Equipment Corporation† sent me this electronic mail: "The author should concentrate on the logical structure of the text more than its visual representation. The nice thing about the typesetting systems you mentioned by name is that they allow the user to do this by defining commands. For example, the author of a cookbook can define logical structures like *Recipe*, *Ingredient List*, and *Preparation Step*. The author can easily change the formatting of these structures by redefining those commands. (A serious problem with many typesetting systems is that they encourage the user not to do this, but instead to add commands like *Add Vertical Space* and *Two-Column List*.)"

Lamport continues, "Some of the advantages of such an approach are obvious. Reformatting a paper from one journal format to another journal format, for instance, is rapid and almost painless. What is less obvious is how this improves the writing by forcing the author to be aware of the document's structure (or lack of structure)."

10.5 The Right Medium

So far this column has concentrated on improving a given kind of presentation. In an important sense, such typographic polishing is inherently superficial. Pretty typography can't rescue a paper from bad spelling, faulty grammar, poor organization, or lack of content. We'll turn now to a fundamental contribution that typography can make to the clarity of a paper. Many ideas can be embodied in several different forms, such as equations, pictures, or tables; modern document production systems give programmers a great deal of freedom in choosing the best form to convey an idea.

---

† Lamport is the author of LATEX, a set of macros that provide a more structured interface to Knuth's TEX typesetting system. He elaborates the ideas in his note in "Document production: visual or logical" in the "Mathematical text processing" column in the June 1987 *Notices* of the American Mathematical Society, pp. 621–624.

In selecting the right medium, we programmers have two important advantages over professional typographers:

Speed. An editor who wishes to experiment in stylistic changes to text must send instructions to a printer (often in a different city) then wait for the printer to do the job and ship back the results. That process takes days, while many programmers can do the job in minutes.

Flexibility. An editor must choose the final form for an idea early in the game then farm the work out to an expert in that area (such as a professional artist). Many programmers have tools that allow them to experiment with different media to present an idea.

The rest of this section experiments with different forms for conveying ideas.

Old geometry books contain sentences like "The square of the hypotenuse of a right triangle is equal to the sum of the squares of the two adjacent sides." We can now communicate that message by combining this picture

with the equation $a^2 = b^2 + c^2$.

There are many ways to prove the Pythagorean theorem. We could use the Euclidean notation found in classical geometry texts (a typographic challenge, but not insurmountable), we could take a more algebraic approach, or we could draw this figure:

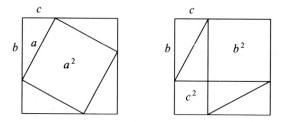

Both squares contain the same four triangles (whose total area is $2bc$). The remaining area is a^2 in the left square and $b^2 + c^2$ in the right square.

Figures don't always reduce space, though. In *Book Design—Systematic Aspects* (Bowker, 1978), Stanley Rice devotes the entirety of page 97 to a graph relating the number of characters in a manuscript to the number of pages in the resulting book. He could have replaced that page with the equation $p = 0.318c$, where p is the number of pages and c is the number of characters in thousands, or with the phrase "3145 characters per page". The best choice in such circumstances depends strongly on the cost of an additional page and the comfort of readers of the book with graphs versus equations.

Section 1.3 profiled a UNIX pipeline for finding the most common words in a document; we'll see a related pipeline in Section 11.1. The heart of the pipeline is a common idiom in the UNIX Shell language:

```
sort | uniq -c | sort -rn
```

The first `sort` gathers together equal words, the `uniq` program removes duplicates and precedes each with a count (the `-c` option), and the second `sort` arranges the words in decreasing order (the flags are to reverse the sort and to use numeric comparisons). Here is the pipeline in pictures, on the input stream "this is this and that is not this":

```
this            and
is              is
this            is          1 and              3 this
and    sort     not  uniq -c 2 is    sort -rn   2 is
that  ------>   that -----> 1 not  ---------->  1 that
is              this        1 that             1 not
not             this        3 this             1 and
this            this
```

Column 15 describes an algorithm for selecting the Kth-largest element in a set. It uses a routine to partition the array $X[L..U]$; the loop invariant can be expressed formally as an equation:

$$X[L] = T \quad \wedge \quad \mathbf{V}_{L+1 \leqslant j \leqslant M}\, X[j] < T \quad \wedge \quad \mathbf{V}_{M+1 \leqslant j \leqslant I-1}\, X[j] \geqslant T$$

One could use a common abbreviation for arrays to express the same facts as comments in a program:

```
X[L] = T   and   X[L+1..M] < T   and   X[M+1..I-1] >= T
```

But I believe that the clearest way to communicate the point to people is by a picture of the array:

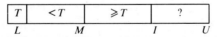

```
| T |  <T  |  ≥T  |   ?   |
  L      M       I       U
```

Solutions 3.1, 3.2, and 3.3 deal with the heap data structure and the Heap-sort algorithm. Both depend on the array $X[L..U]$ having the property *Heap* (L,U), which is defined mathematically as

$$\mathbf{V}_{2L \leqslant i \leqslant U}\, X[i \text{ div } 2] \leqslant X[i]$$

Here is an array in which all subarrays have the heap property:

```
| 12  20  15  29  23  17  22  35  40  26  51  19 |
  1                                            12
```

Heapsort views the array as a binary tree in which $X[I]$ has $X[2I]$ as a left child and $X[2I+1]$ as a right child:

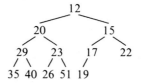

This binary tree is a heap because each node has a value less than the values in its (zero, one or two) children. Problem 2 contains additional questions about the Heapsort algorithm.

In Column 2 we saw Whorf's hypothesis, which states that "Man's thought is shaped by his tongue." For a long time, my documents were shaped by the system on which I wrote them. That system supported only text, so I worked hard to cram my ideas into words. The system I now use lets the content shape the documents: the ideas can find their homes in text, equations, tables, figures, programs, graphs, or many other devices. This software encourages me to be a better author.

And the resulting documents, though laden with displays of various kinds, are gentle on the reader. At natural times, the discussion moves from text to pictures to equations to programs, all dictated by the logical flow. Some journals require that all figures be placed at the end of the paper, which eases production at great expense in readability. Imagine trying to read a mathematical paper in which all equations were numbered, captioned, and herded off to the end, or a programming text in which all code appeared in Appendix 3! Laying out a well-integrated paper is more work for the programmer/author, but it greatly helps the reader, for whom the paper exists in the first place.

10.6 Principles

Whether they like it or not, many programmers are now local experts in document design. That may not be quite as ludicrous as it sounds. Fred Brooks eloquently describes the joys and woes of the programmer's craft in Chapter 1 of his *Mythical Man Month*. Document production shares many of the experiences on his list. Both tasks involve "making things that are useful to other people" and in both "one must perform perfectly". The greatest delight for me is that both yield "the sheer joy of making things".

Document design requires creativity. A library in which all documents looked alike would be as dreadfully boring as a world in which all people dressed the same and all cars had the same body style and color (probably black). The best design depends on many attributes of the document; the package must be tailored to the contents.

But beware of too much creativity. Strunk and White advise authors to

"Place yourself in the background." Good document style, like good programming style or good writing style, is invisible. The content is the primary purpose of the document; the document style is only a means to that end.

10.7 Problems

1. Many mathematical proofs make extensive use of pictures. Choose a proof that is easy to present at a blackboard, and express it in your document production system. Rich candidates include the sum $1+2+...+N$, other properties of Pascal's triangle, and other proofs of the Pythagorean theorem.

2. After building the array $X[1..N]$ into a heap, Heapsort uses this invariant:

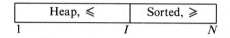

The inequality signs abbreviate $X[1..I] \leqslant X[I+1..N]$. The loop index I proceeds from N down to 2; the sorted portion of the array grows from size 0 to the entire array. Draw pictures to show the progress of Heapsort, as well as other sorts based on selecting the largest element.

3. In *Methods of Book Design* (third edition, Yale University Press, 1983), Hugh Williamson identifies three primary goals for documents: correctness, consistency, and clarity. How should you typeset your computer programs to reach these goals?

10.8 Further Reading

The thirteenth edition of *The Chicago Manual of Style* was published by the University of Chicago Press in 1982. In addition to presenting the house style of that press, the book presents the principles underlying the particular choices. This work is a standard in many publishing houses. Programmers who play publisher would do well to have a copy on their desktop.

10.9 A Catalog of Pet Peeves *[Sidebar]*

Several readers made comments of the form, "You failed to warn about the dreaded...." Many of those warnings have been incorporated into the text, but here are a few minor points to consider.

Wide Text. Try to keep lines at most 75 characters long, including spaces and punctuation. Readers of longer lines tend to lose track when their eyes scan back (left) to the next line. Computer scientists often make this mistake by using a 10-point font on 8.5-inch paper with 1-inch margins.

Low-Resolution Devices. The quality of output improves in the sequence of dot-matrix printers, daisy-wheel printers, laser printers, and phototypesetters; the devices range in price from a few hundred dollars to a few tens of thousand dollars. Once readers are used to one level of quality, it is hard to go back to a lower level.

Underlined Words. An italic font will usually do the job more gracefully but does the job really need to be done at all? There are only a few notations more jarring than underlining.

Typitis. One particularly frustrated reader fantasized that this column would include a sample of output from a popular laser printer, along with his critique: "This laser printer has a resolution of about 300 dots per inch. The fonts were designed by engineers, not type designers. This sample is quite difficult to read because it has too much blackness, the proportions between height and width are imbalanced, white space within letters is imbalanced with white space between letters, it lacks rhythm. However, the ability to mix fonts within a line makes it ideally suited to generating ransom notes."

Truth in Advertising. In the old days, the appearance of a document accurately reflected its status. As the appearance progressed from handwritten notes to typed rough draft to finely typewritten technical report to journal article, the content grew more polished. If your beautifully typeset document contains a few ideas you had over breakfast this morning, please remember to label it as a "rough draft".

Missed Resources. Leslie Lamport of DEC sent this electronic mail, "You omitted the simplest and most effective advice for neophyte designers: go to the bookshelf and look at what real book designers do. (These days, you may have to look at non-computer science books to find one that wasn't typeset by an amateur.) It's amazing how few people think of doing that."

Pictures of Computer Screens. Another reader writes, "These may have verisimilitude, but they offer little else. Screens are usually full of irrelevant stuff. Moreover, screens are inherently cheap, fast and ephemeral. If your document is also, why did you write it down in the first place?"

Dumb Hyphe-nation. Most hyphenation programs do pretty well, but protect your readers from such juicy word breaks as scar-city, the-rapist, and uncle-an.

Double Quotes. "These" double quotes on the keyboard are fine for strings in a program, but "these" belong in text.

Fig. This common abbreviation for figure saves about two-and-a-half characters by looking ugly (oops, I mean, ug.).

Mallory's disease. Mallory tried to climb Mt. Everest "Because it is there." That is a fine reason to climb a mountain, but a dreadful reason to emphasize words with a 24-point sans serif double ugly font.

COLUMN 11: **GRAPHIC OUTPUT**

Computer systems are getting bigger and better every year: they have more memory, faster processors and larger databases. That's good news — computers can store more data and expend more effort processing it. But once a system has performed a massive computation, how can we summarize the trends in the mountain of data?

The answer to that question depends heavily on both the data and the tastes of the reader. Paragraphs of text and tables of numbers often provide fine summaries. This column, however, will concentrate on graphical representations of data, which allow the powerful human vision system to process data. Laser printers and graphics impact printers are widely available at low cost; software packages bring graphical techniques home to most programmers. This column shows how we programmers can use the technology to deliver more useful (and more graphic) output.

11.1 A Case Study

In this section we'll use some simple graphical methods to study one data set. Columns 1 and 2 considered the problem of listing all the words in a file, together with a count of how many times each occurs. Section 2.1 described this Awk program for the task:

```
      { for (i = 1; i <= NF; i++) count[$i]++ }
  END { for (i in count) print count[i], i }
```

This UNIX Shell pipeline performs the same task; it is similar to a program in Section 1.3:

```
  cat $* | tr -s '\t ' '\012' | sort | uniq -c
```

For consistency with the Awk program, the program does not transliterate upper case letters to lower case, nor does it sort the final list of words.

I timed both programs on drafts of the fifteen columns in this book. The first line in the table says that Column 1 had 4351 total words, of which 1579

115

were distinct. The Shell pipeline took 3.2 CPU seconds on a VAX-11/750, while the Awk program took 28.2 seconds.

COLUMN	WORDS		RUN TIME	
	Total	Distinct	Shell	Awk
1	4351	1579	3.2	28.2
2	3863	1406	2.6	26.6
3	3577	1324	2.8	26.5
4	2877	1192	2.3	20.2
5	3544	1548	2.9	23.9
6	3066	1248	2.3	21.7
7	3504	1506	2.7	24.1
8	1288	641	1.1	9.3
9	6740	2233	4.5	42.3
10	6707	2402	4.9	43.3
11	3423	1585	2.8	24.0
12	3329	1331	2.7	21.5
13	2404	870	1.8	15.0
14	5028	1708	3.3	31.6
15	4928	1558	3.3	29.2

This section presents some graphs that highlight certain relationships in this data set. But first take a minute to try to find some trends yourself.

This *scatterplot*† displays the two leftmost columns in the table by showing the Awk run time as a function of the Shell run time:

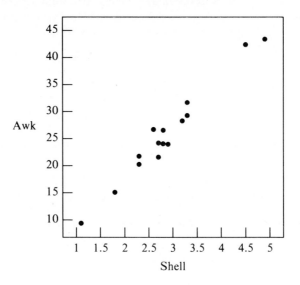

---

† All graphs in this book were produced by "GRAP—A language for typesetting graphs", which Kernighan and I described in the August 1986 *Communications of the ACM*. Grap is implemented as a preprocessor for the Pic language described in Column 9.

The points lie roughly along a line, so I performed a least-squares regression that showed that

$$T_{Awk} = 9.27 \times T_{Shell} - 0.88$$

In words, the Shell program is typically about 9 times faster than the program implemented in the Awk language.

The next graph is a better presentation of the data set. Some of the changes are cosmetic: the graph is slightly smaller, there are fewer ticks, the ticks point outward (ticks within the plotting region tend to obscure the data), and the labels are more informative. Three other changes provide more information: the regression line helps us compare the values to the regression, the larger graphical area shows the regression line passing near the origin, and the plotting symbols are the column numbers.

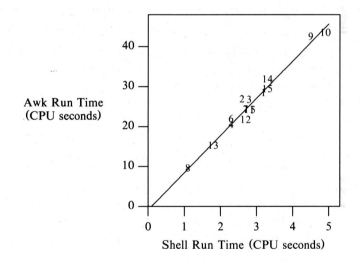

Notice that all columns lie near the line, which passes close to the origin. Little Column 8 is processed very quickly, while big Columns 9 and 10 take much more CPU time.

The next pair of graphs show some relationships between distinct words, total words, and run time. The graphs highlight the least-squares regressions

$$W_{Distinct} = 0.29 \times W_{Total} + 343$$

$$T_{Awk} = 0.006 \times W_{Total} + 2.56$$

To conserve space, the displays are shrunk to be a bit smaller and are placed side-by-side:

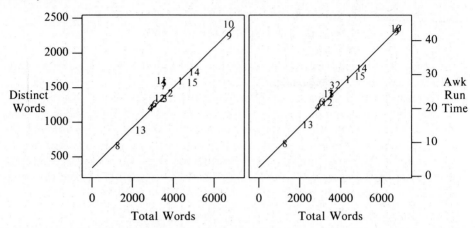

The left graph shows that the number of distinct words is roughly 30% the number of total words, but only roughly. The right graph shows that the Awk run time is quite close to the six seconds per thousand words predicted by the least-squares regression.

11.2 A Sampler of Displays

The last section used one kind of display — scatterplots — to illustrate one data set. In this section we'll survey other kinds of graphs that are more suitable for summarizing other kinds of data.

You don't always need a fancy output device to make a good display. John Tukey's *stem-and-leaf* display, for instance, can be produced on any line printer. This example presents the age at inauguration of the first forty Presidents of the United States (Washington through Reagan; Grover Cleveland is counted twice). The first line records the two ages 42 (Theodore Roosevelt) and 43 (Kennedy); the last line records ages 65 (Buchanan), 68 (Harrison) and 69 (Reagan).

```
40-44 ┆ 23
45-49 ┆ 67899
50-54 ┆ 001111224444
55-59 ┆ 555566677778
60-64 ┆ 011124
65-69 ┆ 589
```

The shape of the display is a histogram of the ages (and bell-shaped at that). Using the units digit as the plotting symbol presents the complete data set.

A *time series* shows how one variable changes over time. The following pair of graphs, for instance, share the x-axis to show how the number of telephones in the United States increased from 1.3 million in 1900 to 120 million in 1970 (the units are millions of telephones, or, obviously, "megaphones").

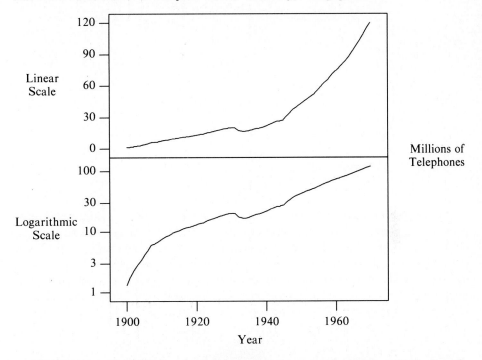

The number of telephones in the country grew at a dramatic rate during the first decade of this century, and then increased at an almost constant percentage rate during the next six decades. There are just two exceptions to that long-term trend. The Great Depression led to a decrease in telephones in the early 1930's, but that dip was made up for by a growth spurt during the Post-War Boom in the late 1940's.

The linear scale on the y-axis in the top graph highlights the rapid growth after 1940, but hides much of the story by squeezing three fifths of the data into the bottom fifth of the graph. The logarithmic scale in the bottom graph highlights the growth rate of telephones; straight lines on log-linear graphs correspond to geometric rates (see Problem 4 and its solution).

The next figure is a variation of Bill Cleveland's *dotchart*, an alternative to the popular bar chart. It combines graphical and tabular methods to display data from Ritchie and Thompson's paper "The UNIX Time-Sharing System", which appeared in the July 1974 *Communications of the ACM*. The table lists all system commands that account for more than two percent of either CPU time or command invocations. The data on CPU time could be useful for reducing run time (it is a higher level profile than those we saw in Column 1), while the data on command invocations could be useful for designing user interfaces. In both categories fewer than ten commands accounted for over half the usage.

C compiler ·15.7	Editor ·15.3
User program ·15.2	List directory · · · · · · · · · · · · 9.6
Editor · · · · · · · · · · · · · · · ·11.7	C compiler · · · · · · · · 6.3
Shell · · · · · · · 5.8	Remove file · · · · · · · · 6.3
Chess · · · · · · · 5.3	User program · · · · · · · · 6.0
List directory · · · · 3.3	Print file · · · · · · · · 6.0
Troff · · · · 3.1	List users · · · · 3.3
Backup · · · 2.6	Move file · · · · 3.2
	File status · · · · 3.1

0 5 10 15	0 5 10 15
Percent of CPU Usage	Percent of Command Accesses
(Top 8 account for 62.7%)	(Top 9 account for 59.1%)

Many graphics systems make it easy to present data like this in the ever-popular pie chart. That is unfortunate, because dot charts are almost always a better way to present such data. My personal taste is backed up by experiments that show that the human eye can compare lengths more effectively than it can compare angles. In fairness, though, pie charts are sometimes effective. The September 1987 *Princeton Engineer* used this graph to report the (alleged) responses to the question "Is Princeton too homogeneous?"

No 100%

Pie charts are fine for the number "100%"; dot charts are better for more complex data sets.

Different data sets call for different kinds of displays; here are the graphical displays of data sets used throughout this book:

SECTION	GRAPHICAL DISPLAY
10.3	Direction field
11.2	Scatterplot
11.3	Stem-and-leaf display
11.3	Time series
11.3	Dotchart
11.6	Time series on a map
12.2	Bar chart
12.2	Histogram
14.8	Multiple time series
15.3	Box-and-whiskers display

11.3 Principles

Effective graphs require a diverse set of skills. The author of a graph must understand the application well enough to know what data should be summarized, must appreciate enough statistics to avoid drawing unwarranted (or just plain wrong) conclusions, and must design and execute the graph in the chosen medium (be it India ink or laser printer). This section will enumerate several principles relevant to these activities; most of the principles are taken from one or more of the references.

The Strengths of Graphs. Graphs can portray a complex set of relationships simply and clearly. They are most effective when they are processed by the eyes rather than the brain; that is, the reader of a graph should use the vision system more than cognitive skills. Graphs should be designed to show the structure of and the relationships among data; they should rarely be used to present details. Graphs in a computer system should therefore summarize details that are also presented elsewhere.

Statistical Integrity. The primary requirement of any form of professional communication is accuracy. The first concern of a graph is therefore its content: Are the measurements appropriate? Are the trends that you highlighted in the graph statistically significant? Is the data biased by tainted sampling? The form of the graph can also mislead: Is it labelled properly? Are the symbols that plot the data of size proportional to the data? Huff's *How to Lie with Statistics* delightfully sketches these issues.

Beauty. Graphs should excite the reader's interest in the data. To do this, they must be attractive. On the other hand, the purpose of a graph is to show the data, not to draw attention to itself. An elegant graph is therefore a simple design that illuminates complex data. Effective methods for achieving appealing graphs include starting with a simple (and preferably well known) form and erasing superfluous ink.

The Process. Superlative graphs do not spring from programmers' foreheads; they are usually the result of several iterations of a three-phase sequence. In the exploratory phase, preliminary graphs ignore cosmetic issues entirely and concentrate on showing trends in the data. Next, a confirmatory phase uses elementary statistics (or at least common sense) to make sure that the trends are significant. The presentation phase selects the final form of the graph and executes it in the appropriate medium.

Don't Overdo It. In the old days graphs were so hard to make that we almost never used them. Today we suffer from the opposite problem: graphics packages are so easy to use that they can tempt a programmer to graph abuse. Why would you bother writing the simple phrase that "51.27% of the babies

born in the United States in 1980 were males" when you could instead plop
down this marvelous graph?

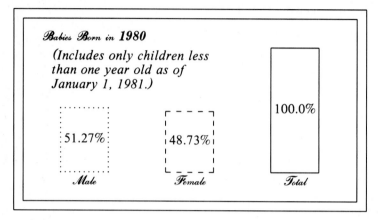

The future is bright for computer-generated graphical display of data. Don't
give it a bad name.

11.4 Problems

1. Experiment with different presentations of data. Consider issues like these.

   a. *Medium.* Are graphs the best form for the data? Should it be presented
   in text or tables instead?

   b. *Form.* Have you chosen the best graphical display? Should your data be
   presented in a scatterplot, histogram, or time series? Are the right variables plotted? For instance, should the telephone graph show the number
   of telephones each year or the ratio of telephones this year to telephones
   last year? How could you plot additional information to study, say, telephones per capita? Should the scales be linear, logarithmic, or use some
   other transformation?

   c. *Execution.* What is the best local structure for the graph? Should scatterplots and time series plots have a background grid rather than ticks on
   the axes? How many tick marks and where? What labels should mark
   the axes?

2. [E. Tufte] Clutter on a graph distracts from the data. Try deleting some of
   the components of a graph. If you don't have a computerized system available, try making several xerographic copies of a graph and use white
   "correction fluid" to erase excess material. Experiment until you find the
   balance you like best. I found this to be particularly useful when applied to
   my own graphs: the simpler graphs were more attractive at first glance and
   presented the data more forcefully.

3. [P. A. Tukey] *Graphical Methods for Data Analysis* by Chambers, Cleveland, Kleiner and Tukey was published in 1983 by Wadsworth International Group (the paperback version was published by Duxbury Press). Appendix 7 summarizes thirteen attributes of 74 automobiles as sold in the United States in the 1979 model year. Rather than presenting a list of 74 mileage and weight pairs, the following table gives the mileage in the first column and weights of all cars with that mileage in later columns. The first line says that two automobiles were rated at 12 miles per gallon; their weights were 4720 and 4840 pounds.

```
12    4720 4840
13
14    3420 3830 3900 4060 4130 4330
15    3720 4080
16    3690 3870 3880 4030
17    2830 3170 3350 3740
18    2410 2670 3330 3370 3470 3600 3670 3690 3700
19    3200 3210 3300 3310 3370 3400 3420 3430
20    2830 3250 3280
21    2130 2650 2750 4060 4290
22    2580 2640 2930 3180 3220
23    2070 2160 2370
24    2280 2690 2720 2750
25    1930 1990 2200 2240 2650
26    1830 2230 2520
27
28    1760 1800 2360
29    2110
30    1980 2120
31    2200
32
33
34    1800
35    2020 2050
36
37
38
39
40
41    2040
```

In addition to presenting the data set, this figure is also a histogram similar to the stem-and-leaf display in Section 11.2. Explore the relationship between weight and mileage.

4. Explain why the relation $y=a \times x^b$ plots as a straight line when both x and y use logarithmic scales. Explain why $y=a \times b^x$ plots as a line when x uses a linear scale and y uses a logarithmic scale. How are a and b reflected in the plots? What scales would you use to present the relationship $y=a\sqrt{x}+b$?

5. Write a program that graphically displays the output of your system random number generator. The simplest display divides the generator's domain into equal-sized bins and then displays a histogram of the count of random numbers in each bin. Although a visual display is sufficient to identify grossly inadequate generators, consult Section 3.3 of Knuth's *Seminumerical Algorithms* before you criticize a marginal generator.

11.5 Further Reading

One can argue that Darrell Huff's *How to Lie with Statistics* (published in 1954 by W. W. Norton and Company, NY, but reprinted often) should be required for anyone who reads either the popular media or the technical literature. It describes various ways to slant graphs to make a point, and equips you with questions to ask about a graph. But all argument ends when you are summarizing data yourself; you must read this charming little book. It contains simple but effective principles for valid statistical summaries and for presenting a summary in graphical form.

Edward Tufte's *Visual Display of Quantitative Information* is handsome decoration for any coffee table and great motivation for any programmer. The book assumes that you have already summarized the data and concentrates on principles of graphical design and integrity. The graphic of Napoleon's Russian campaign in Section 11.6 is a sample of Tufte's collection of graphical excellence spanning the eighteenth, nineteenth and twentieth centuries. The book is available only directly from the publisher; its price is $34.00 postpaid from Graphics Press, Box 430, Cheshire, Connecticut 06410.

Bill Cleveland's *Elements of Graphing Data* was published by Wadsworth in 1985. He describes fundamental principles of constructing graphs and surveys many graphical methods, classified by the kind of data they display. Fascinating data sets and marvelous graphs make for delightful browsing, and the graphical principles merit careful study. If you are going to present and analyze data in graphical displays, this book is for you.

11.6 Napoleon's March to Moscow *[Sidebar]*

How would you summarize Napoleon's disastrous Russian campaign of 1812? Many programmers would be tempted to produce several inches of line printer output giving a day-by-day account of personnel, supplies and location complete with weekly and monthly subtotals highlighted by asterisks. The French engineer Charles Joseph Minard took a different approach to the problem in 1861: he summarized the campaign in a single graphic. Edward Tufte expresses the popular opinion that, "It may well be the best statistical graphic ever drawn." I spent a pleasant afternoon rendering a slightly updated version of Minard's graphic in the Pic language.

The upper band shows the route of Napoleon's main force from the crossing of the Niemen River on 23 June 1812 to the occupation of Moscow on 14 September. The width of the band is proportional to the size of the army (reduced from 422,000 men to 100,000). The lower (dark) band shows the size of the army during its retreat, from late October to 26 December when 10,000 survivors straggled across the Niemen. Two movements to protect the French flanks are similarly displayed. The numbers near the bands give the size of the forces in thousands of troops. The graph at the bottom is read right-to-left; it shows certain low temperatures and dates during the retreat.

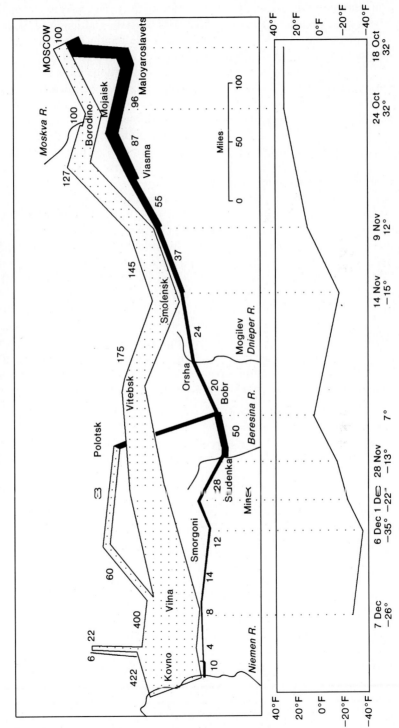

NAPOLEON'S RUSSIAN CAMPAIGN: June to December, 1812

This graphic relates six distinct variables against the background of the cities and rivers on a map: the army's position (its latitude and longitude), its size, its direction of movement, the temperature, and the date. Together they describe the destruction of an army and the beginning of the end of an empire.

The Russian strategy was primarily one of attrition, but the graphic shows several major battles. Borodino on 7 September was claimed as a victory by both sides. The Russians nearly devastated the rear half of the French army at Viasma on 3 November, and Krasnoe (near Smolensk) saw a running battle for four days on 15–18 November. The graphic highlights the deadly crossing of the Beresina River at Studenka on 26–28 November: a thaw a few days earlier gorged the river, and the temperature dropped to brutal extremes for the crossing itself and the remainder of the retreat.

The prominent role of temperature in this graph suggests its French origin. The Russian winter was in fact fairly mild until the cold spell of the last week in November, at which time the French army was already obliterated. French accounts of the campaign, starting with the reports of Napoleon himself, blame the disaster on the cold; Russian descriptions tend not to focus on the weather.

I kept the primary structure of Minard's graphic, including all of his numbers (even a few of dubious accuracy). I made several cosmetic changes: towns are labelled by their modern names, the scale is in miles rather than common leagues, the temperatures use Fahrenheit's scale rather than Réaumur's, and dates are in English. (As a geographical aid, the city of Kovno is in Lithuania, about 50 miles northeast of the modern Polish border and 500 miles west of Moscow.) Tufte reprints Minard's original graphic and describes it with verve and appreciation on pages 40 and 41 of his *Visual Display of Quantitative Information*.

COLUMN 12: **A SURVEY OF SURVEYS**

Everybody knows about surveys. The press bombards us with poll results ranging from the President's popularity to preferences among brands of popcorn. In 1980 I had a chance to learn a little about the mechanism behind those surveys. I installed personal computers in a polling firm and wrote programs to automate some of the firm's activities.

The first section of this column gives a brief background on polling. The next two sections sketch two interesting pieces of the system. The second section discusses a little language for describing surveys, and the third section describes some techniques for graphical display of data that were incorporated into the company's reports.

Columns 9, 10 and 11 describe general principles for making computer input and output fit for human consumption. They illustrate the principles with examples that might appear rather exotic to some programmers. This column therefore applies the techniques to a mundane data processing system implemented in the Basic language on a microcomputer.

12.1 The Problems of Polling

I installed the company's first on-site computers in late 1980: three 48-kilobyte microcomputers. Some of the tasks to be automated were common to all small businesses, such as preparing a payroll. Many of the tasks, though, were quite specialized to polling. Solution 3 in Section 5.2, for instance, describes a simple program that was useful in drawing random samples.

What follows is a grossly oversimplified sketch of polling. I'll give only the ideas that are necessary for understanding the interesting issues in language design and data presentation. There are three primary data processing problems to be faced:

Input: At some time a human interviewer asks questions of a respondent. Some organizations administer the survey using a paper questionnaire; the responses are later manually keyed into a database. Other organizations administer questions by computers that record the responses online.

Validation: There are many checks for consistency and completeness. Some issues are global: Is each respondent counted exactly once in the database? Other checks deal with a single record: Are all questions answered and all responses in a valid range? Are "Democrat Only" questions administered to all and only Democrats?

Tabulation and Output: Once the questionnaire database is complete, the responses are tabulated and presented in a final report. The body of the report is a one-page description for each question. Other material includes a cover page, table of contents, description of survey methods, and a summary of primary trends.

The next section shows how little languages are useful in all three tasks, and the subsequent section describes some graphical techniques that were incorporated into the final report.

12.2 The Languages

The system I built has three "generic" programs, one for each of the primary tasks. The programs are specialized to a particular survey by a description written in a little language, which I'll call BPL for "Basic Polling Language". Here is the first part of a BPL description of a survey:

```
Q1,5 What is your political party?
   1 Democrat
   2 Republican
   3 Other
Q2,6 For whom did you vote in 1984?
   1 Reagan/Bush
   2 Mondale/Ferraro
   3 Named Other Candidate
   4 Didn't Vote
   5 Don't Know
Q3,7 Where is your polling place?
   1 Named a place
   2 Did not name a place
Q4,8 In this election, are you
   1 Very interested
   2 Somewhat interested
   3 Not interested
```

Each line that begins with a "Q" describes a question: Question 1, for instance, is stored in column 5 of each record, and asks the respondent's political party. The next three lines are the three possible responses to the question. Allowing the user to indent the responses under the question makes the file easier to read.

The single BPL language serves as the input language for the three different generic programs.

Input: An interactive program can administer the survey from a BPL description and store the results in the database. If an organization uses paper questionnaires, then the BPL file can be read by a "pretty-print" program to prepare the master copy of the questionnaire and by a data-entry program to describe record formats.

Validation: From a BPL description, a program can ensure that all questions are answered and that all responses are in a legal range. We'll see shortly how another little language can be used to check more subtle constraints.

Tabulation and Output: The BPL description provides the bulk of the input to the program that produces the final report of a survey. The user specifies in yet another simple language the titles to appear on the report, which questions should be cross-tabulated, and headings for the cross-tabulations.

Just as a Fortran description of a computation can be compiled and executed on many kinds of computers, a single BPL description of a survey can be interpreted to perform several different tasks.

I have neglected a ton of details that complicate all survey programs. For instance, even though the questions were asked in one order, the user might want them to appear on the output in a different order (say, from greatest to least frequency of response). We'll see several other complications shortly. When I first designed the program, I sketched half a dozen bells and whistles before I realized that such was the way of folly: I could never anticipate all the options a user might desire, and any program that dealt with all options would be a rat's nest of code.

I therefore looked for a general mechanism that could handle the problems, and finally settled on a construct I called *pseudocolumns*. The "real" data was stored in columns 1 through 250 of the input record. As each record is read, the program generates pseudocolumns starting at column 251. The user defines pseudocolumns in a second little language. The BPL description we saw earlier states that column 5 contains party information in the order Democrat, Republican, Other. To print Republicans before Democrats, one could define column 251 as follows:

```
define 251
    1 if 5 is 2   # Republican
    2 if 5 is 1   # Democrat
    3 otherwise   # Other
```

As in Pic, the # character introduces a comment. The user can now refer to column 251:

```
Q1,251 What is your political party?
    1 Republican
    2 Democrat
    3 Other
```

Another common task is collapsing fields. For instance, the user might wish to collapse the three age brackets 21–25, 26–30 and 31–35 into the single bracket 21–35. If column 19 contains age in 5-year clumps, one can make coarser grains in pseudocolumn 252:

```
define 252     # age, bigger lumps
    1 if 19 is 1        # below 21
    2 if 19 is 2,3,4    # 21-35
    3 if 19 is 5,6,7    # 36-50
    4 otherwise         # over 50
```

Pseudocolumns have a more sophisticated application in identifying "high-propensity" voters, who are most likely to show up at the polls:

```
define 253     # 1 if high-propensity
    1 if 6 is 1,2,3 and 7 is 1 and 8 is 1,2
    2 otherwise
```

This column is one if and only if the respondent remembered his or her 1984 candidate (column 6), could name his or her polling place (column 7), and is interested in this election (column 8). This illustrates the most complex form for a pseudocolumn; it is similar to the "conjunctive normal form" found in boolean algebra.

Pseudocolumns have handled all the problems I knew about during the design phase and many others that I never would have dreamed of. Although the mechanism is quite general, it was easy to implement. The descriptions are read and stored by 90 lines of Basic code, and are interpreted by just 11 lines of Basic code.

There are many ways to process survey data without using little languages. Before I designed this system, I skimmed a college-level textbook on processing and analyzing public opinion surveys. The authors describe the problems of input, validation, and tabulation, and suggest writing a new program from scratch for each task for each survey. They even provide flowcharts and sample Fortran code. That approach might work in a college (it would certainly provide employment for generations of computer science majors), but it is out of the question for a small company.

At one point I seriously considered building an interactive program. It sounded easy at first: tell me the question, tell me the responses, now to the next question. As I explored further, though, I realized that I was designing large portions of a text editor. (I want to change part of question 35. Which part? A response. Which response? 3, I think, but let me see them all. Oops, 4. Change "Smith" to "Smythe", and leave the rest alone....) I finally made progress by abandoning the interactive approach and thinking about the problem as designing a little language to describe surveys (and leaving the editing to the standard text editor!).

Once a programmer has settled on the general approach, there remains the task of designing the little language. The company I worked for had previously used a generic tabulation program that read both its input and the questionnaire

data base from punched cards. The survey described earlier would be presented
to that program as follows:

```
QS0053001What is your political party?
QS0063002For whom did you vote in 1984?
QS0073003Where is your polling place?
QS0083004In this election, are you
ST0052001Democrat
ST0052002Republican
ST0052003Other
ST0062001Reagan/Bush
ST0062002Mondale/Ferraro
ST0062003Named Other Candidate
ST0062004Didn't Vote
ST0062005Don't Know
ST0072001Named a place
ST0072002Did not name a place
ST0082001Very interested
ST0082002Somewhat interested
ST0082003Not interested
ST0054004Total Responses
ST0064006Total Responses
ST0074003Total Responses
ST0084004Total Responses
```

Lines that begin with "QS" describe a question, and "ST" or "stub" lines
denote a response. The mysterious 2's, 3's and 4's encode some of the bells and
whistles handled in my program by pseudocolumns.

Little languages are not all created equal. This one made life easy for the
programmer (who wrote in assembly language, in case you couldn't guess) but
difficult for the user. The BPL language contains almost the same information,
but in a more rational format. This description has all questions precede all
answers, the way the machine stores them. BPL places them the way the user
thinks of them, with the responses right after the question. This description
uses vile fixed-column input; BPL uses free-format input, which humans deserve.
Since all questions have a "Total Responses" line, BPL supplies it.

The linguistic view made the new program easier to use than its mainframe
predecessor. It took employees about two working days with a card punch to
describe a survey for the old program, and several computer runs to debug it.
The same job takes just two hours with the new program, and most inputs run
the first time.

12.3 The Pictures

When the firm conducts a survey, it has a lot of data to summarize. A typical political study polls, say, eight hundred respondents and asks seventy questions of each. The main body of the final report contains one page for each
question, with percentages on the various answers for the entire population and
for certain subpopulations, such as Republicans, Democrats, males, and females.

Although some details are of great interest, the sheer bulk of the report is a barrier to many readers. The report therefore has a brief "overview" section. I'll now sketch the original overview and its new, graphical form.

Before summarizing data one must decide what trends the reader wants to see. Typical political clients care about such issues as geographical areas of strength and comparison with past perceptions. This section will focus on a dimension that attracted a great deal of media attention in the mid-1980's: the "gender gap" between the political opinions of men and women. The data is from a late-1983 poll of 800 voters in the State of New Mexico.

One series of questions concerned the potential 1984 presidential race between incumbent Republican President Ronald Reagan and several possible Democratic candidates. (For whom would you vote if Reagan were to run against Mondale? Against Glenn? Against Hart?) The data on several pages of the report had previously been summarized in a one-page, typewritten table:

	Reagan	Democrat	Don't Know
Walter Mondale			
Total	49.4%	36.6%	14.0%
Male	58.1%	30.3%	11.7%
Female	40.6%	43.1%	16.4%
John Glenn			
Total	48.0%	38.4%	13.5%
Male	54.6%	34.7%	10.7%
Female	41.3%	42.1%	16.6%
Gary Hart			
Total	50.8%	28.4%	20.8%
Male	58.1%	25.3%	16.6%
Female	43.3%	31.5%	25.2%

The first line of the table indicates that 49.4% of the respondents preferred Reagan in a Reagan-Mondale race while 36.6% preferred Mondale and 14.0% didn't know. The next line gives similar percentages for male respondents. The above data is now presented graphically in a group of bar charts:

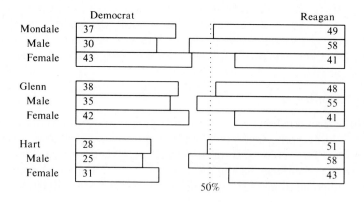

The dotted line is at the 50% level needed to win the election. The gaps between the bars reflect the "don't know" respondents.

Although the facts are present in both representations, the graph highlights several trends. First, at the time and place of the poll, President Reagan was in a very strong position. His strength in the total population was right at the fifty percent needed to carry the state, he had overwhelming strength among males, and even among females he was quite close to Mondale and Glenn, and stronger than Hart. A gender gap is evident both in the support of the president and in a larger "Don't Know" factor among females.

Bar charts are not a fancy graphical device, but they are fine for this job. Because they are well known, they are comfortable for almost all readers. Their simple form makes them easy to specify in yet another little language and easy to implement on an inexpensive impact printer with a graphics character set.

Another series of questions asked the respondents to rate the overall job performance of several elected officials. The old overview summarized the responses in a table of percentages; the new overview section gives them in the following graph.

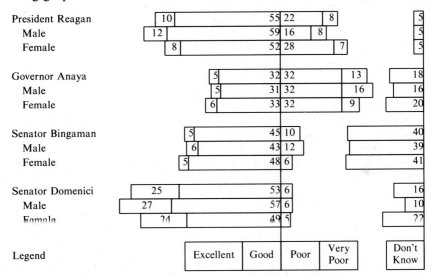

The second line indicates that 12% of males rated President Reagan's performance as "Excellent", 59% rated him as "Good", and so forth. Both Senators received "Very Poor" ratings of two percent or less, so those responses are lumped in with "Poor".

This series of bar charts reveals several trends. Governor Anaya was mildly unpopular at the time. Senator Bingaman was not well known but was popular among those who did know him. Almost everyone expressed an opinion about President Reagan and most were pleased with his performance. Senator Domenici had wildly enthusiastic support from his constituents. The only gender gap seems to be in the perception of President Reagan and in one larger "Don't Know" factor among females.

Like any other data, polls must be understood in context. They reflect the opinion only of the population sampled and only at a particular time. The sampling itself introduces error. A sentence in the old report declared that "The sample size of 800 gives a 95% confidence interval of plus or minus 3.4%." The new report amplifies that as follows.

One hundred computer experiments were conducted to illustrate the sampling process. Each experiment tossed 800 fair coins (by computer simulation) and recorded the percentage of heads; this corresponds to sampling 800 voters from New Mexico and asking their opinions on a 50%-50% issue. The results were

```
     <46.5% (  0)
  46.5-47.4 (  1) X
  47.5-48.4 ( 13) XXXXXXXXXXXXX
  48.5-49.4 ( 22) XXXXXXXXXXXXXXXXXXXXXX
  49.5-50.4 ( 21) XXXXXXXXXXXXXXXXXXXXX
  50.5-51.4 ( 27) XXXXXXXXXXXXXXXXXXXXXXXXXXX
  51.5-52.4 ( 11) XXXXXXXXXXX
  52.5-53.4 (  5) XXXXX
     >53.4% (  0)
```

The middle line says that of the 100 experiments, 21 had a percentage of heads from 49.5% to 50.4%. Seventy percent of the experiments were within 1.5% of the true answer and all experiments were within 3.5% of the true answer; we can expect similar accuracy from the poll.

The histogram can be produced on a line printer without graphics capabilities. Clients have reported that the explanation gives them a good intuitive feeling for the 3.4% confidence interval.

The old overview section of the report consisted of about ten tables of percentages, one table per page. The new overview also has ten pages, but now each page presents its data graphically. The graphs are more expensive to prepare: the tables required a couple of secretarial hours, while the graphics require about twice that.

Are graphs worth two extra hours? In-house analysts think so: because of their familiarity with the graphs, they can see trends at a glance. Regular clients also find the graphs helpful; comparing the new graphs with the last set is easy to do visually and shows important changes over the interim. Even one-time clients find the graphs useful after a minute or two of browsing. An intangible benefit is that the graphs make the report look a little more exciting. The bottom line is that the company has done away with the tables and now uses only graphs in the overviews.

12.4 Principles

Columns 9, 10 and 11 describe general principles for the design of input/output and illustrate them in colorful contexts. This column has applied the same principles to a more drab data processing environment, with results that were far from drab for the company.

Little Languages. Most of the languages in Column 9 were designed by and for programmers. Programmers spend their lives with languages; they can excuse awkward syntax here and there, but they demand the power of programmability. The languages in Section 12.2 were designed for users with no background in computing. I therefore bent over backwards to design languages that would be simple to learn and easy to use.

Graphic Output. Most of the graphics in Column 11 can be produced only on sophisticated printers driven by advanced software. The bar charts in Section 12.3 were easy to render on a simple impact printer that sold for a couple hundred dollars. And I stuck to a simple and well-known graphical form; no logarithmic scales for these users!

12.5 Problems

1. These questions deal with the BPL language for describing surveys.

   a. The example incorrectly assumed that a question or a response always fits on a single line. Extend the language to handle multiple-line text.

   b. The response numbers are redundant, because they always appear in the order 1, 2, 3, ... The program could have supplied them; why did the language insist that the user provide the numbers?

   c. Design a program to automate the administration of a survey. Describe a mechanism to ensure, for instance, that Democrat-only questions are asked only of Democrats.

2. The pseudocolumns in Section 12.2 were designed to make common conditions easy to specify. It is possible to describe other conditions, but with greater difficulty. Suppose that columns 25 and 33 both contain values in the range 1..4; write a pseudocolumn that is 1 if the two columns contain the same value and 2 otherwise.

3. Use the techniques sketched in Problem 11.1 to improve the graphs in this column. Consider issues like the following.

   a. *Medium.* Are graphs the best form for the data? On page 179 of his *Visual Display of Quantitative Information*, cited in Section 11.5, Tufte argues that "super-tables" of percentages are more appropriate for data like polls. (The table he shows is much larger than those in this column — it contains 410 percentages.) In your opinion, which way tells the story more clearly?

b. *Form.* An eager employee at the company redrew the first graph in Section 12.3 to have this form. Compare the new graph to the original. Which is best, and why?

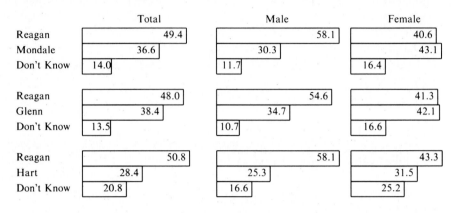

	Total	Male	Female
Reagan	49.4	58.1	40.6
Mondale	36.6	30.3	43.1
Don't Know	14.0	11.7	16.4
Reagan	48.0	54.6	41.3
Glenn	38.4	34.7	42.1
Don't Know	13.5	10.7	16.6
Reagan	50.8	58.1	43.3
Hart	28.4	25.3	31.5
Don't Know	20.8	16.6	25.2

c. *Execution.* What is the best local structure for the graph? For instance, do the percentages in the bar charts help or hinder?

PART IV: **ALGORITHMS**

Aeronautical engineers have their paper airplanes, structural engineers have their balsa wood bridges, and we programmers have our little subroutines. Every now and then they are useful in real programs, but they always teach us more about our craft as programmers.

Communications of the ACM publishes three different kinds of descriptions of programs. "Case Studies" sketch substantial computer systems, such as an airline reservation system or NASA's manned space flight software. "Literate Programming" presents the complete listing of programs that fit in a few pages. These "Programming Pearls" columns contain a more exhaustive description of microscopic subroutines.

Column 13 describes Bob Floyd's algorithms for generating random combinations and permutations. Column 14 uses techniques of numerical analysis to build an efficient routine for computing Euclidean distances. Column 15 addresses a fundamental problem on ordered sets: selecting the Kth-smallest member of a set.

Column 13 was originally published in *Communications of the ACM* in August 1986, Column 14 appeared in December 1986, and Column 15 appeared in November 1985.

COLUMN 13:   **A SAMPLE OF BRILLIANCE**

How can a computer deal a poker hand? If we assign each card in the deck its own integer between 1 and 52, then we can make a hand from a "random sample" of 5 integers in the range 1..52, for instance,

    4 8 31 46 47

(It is important that no number appear twice; I understand that holding more than one ace of spades can seriously jeopardize a card player's health.) Random samples also arise in applications as diverse as simulation, program testing, and statistics.

The first section of this column reviews several standard algorithms for random sampling. The next section describes an elegant new algorithm by Bob Floyd (when this column first appeared in *Communications of the ACM*, Floyd's name was on the byline as the "Special Guest Oyster"). The third section then describes how Floyd extends his algorithm to generate random permutations of integers.

13.1 A Sampling of Sampling Algorithms

Before we can generate a random sample, we have to be able to generate a single random number. We will therefore assume that we have a function RandInt(L,U) that returns an integer uniformly distributed over $L..U$.†

It is easy to generate a random sequence of M integers in the range 1..N, so long as we don't mind duplicates:

```
for I := 1 to M do
    print RandInt(1, N)
```

---

† If you don't have a *RandInt* function, you can make one using a function *Rand* that returns a random real distributed uniformly in [0,1) by the expression $L+int\,(Rand\times(U+1-L))$. In the unlikely event that your system doesn't even have that routine, consult Knuth's *Seminumerical Algorithms*. But whether you use a system routine or make your own, be careful that *RandInt* returns a value in the range $L..U$ — a value out of range is a nasty bug.

139

When I invoked that program with M set to 12 and N set to 3, the code produced the sequence

```
3  1  3  3  1  1  1  2  1  1  3  1
```

This very sequence might come in handy for your next tough game of rock-paper-scissors. More serious applications include testing finite state machines and testing sorting programs (see Section 3.3).

Many applications, though, require a random sample without duplicates. A statistical analysis, for instance, might waste work by observing the same element twice. Such samples are often referred to as "samples without replacement" or as "combinations". For the remainder of this column, though, the word "sample" will denote a random sample with no duplicates. Solution 3 in Section 5.2 describes an application of a program like this.

Many sampling algorithms are based on this pseudocode, which we'll call Algorithm S:

```
initialize set S to empty
Size := 0
while Size < M do
    T := RandInt(1, N)
    if T is not in S then
        insert T in S
        Size := Size + 1
```

The algorithm stores the sample in the set S. If S is implemented correctly and if `RandInt` produces random integers, then the algorithm produces a random sample. That is, each M-element subset is produced with probability $1/\binom{N}{M}$. The loop invariant is that S always contains a random sample of $Size$ integers in the range $1..N$.

There are four operations on the set S: initializing it to empty, testing an integer for membership, inserting a new integer, and printing all the members. Column 11 of my 1986 book *Programming Pearls* sketches the algorithm and five data structures that can be used to implement the set S: bit vectors, unsorted arrays, sorted arrays, binary search trees, and bins. It also sketches several other algorithms for sampling; see Problem 9.

13.2 Floyd's Algorithm

Algorithm S has many virtues: it is correct, fairly efficient, and remarkably succinct. It is so good, as a matter of fact, that I thought one couldn't do better. I therefore charged ahead and described it in detail in a column.

Unfortunately, I was wrong; fortunately, Bob Floyd caught me sleeping. When he studied Algorithm S, he was bothered by a flaw that is displayed clearly when $M=N=100$. When $Size=99$, the set S contains all but one of the desired integers. The algorithm closes its eyes and blindly guesses integers until it stumbles over the right one, which requires 100 random numbers on the average. That analysis assumes that the random number generator is truly random. For some nonrandom sequences, the algorithm won't even terminate.

Floyd set out to find an algorithm that uses exactly one call of `RandInt` for each random number in S. The structure of Floyd's algorithm is easy to understand recursively: to generate a 5-element sample from 1..10, we first generate a 4-element sample from 1..9, and then add the fifth element. The recursive algorithm is sketched as Algorithm F1:

```
function Sample(M, N)
    if M = 0 then
        return the empty set
    else
        S := Sample(M-1, N-1)
        T := RandInt(1, N)
        if T is not in S then
            insert T in S
          else
            insert N in S
        return S
```

We can appreciate the correctness of Algorithm F1 anecdotally. When $M=5$ and $N=10$, the algorithm first recursively computes in S a 4-element random sample from 1..9. Next it assigns to T a random integer in the range 1..10. Of the 10 values that T can assume, exactly 5 result in inserting 10 into S: the four values already in S, and the value 10 itself. Thus element 10 is inserted into the set with the correct probability of 5/10. The next section proves that Algorithm F1 produces each M-element sample of an N-set with equal probability.

Because Algorithm F1 uses a restricted form of recursion, Floyd was able to translate it to an iterative form by introducing a new variable, J. (Problem 8 and Section 3.2 discuss the problem of recursion removal in more general terms.) The result is Algorithm F2, which is more efficient than Algorithm S yet almost as succinct:

```
initialize set S to empty
for J := N - M + 1 to N do
    T := RandInt(1, J)
    if T is not in S then
        insert T in S
      else
        insert J in S
```

Problems 2 and 3 address the data structures that might be used to implement the set S.

For those who might scoff that Algorithm F2 is "just pseudocode", the next program implements Floyd's algorithm in the Awk language. The associative arrays described in Column 2 provide a clean implementation of the set S.

Awk's ARGV array allows the program to access command line arguments, so a sample of 200 elements in the range 1..1000 can be generated by typing sample 200 1000. Complete with input and output, the Awk program requires only eight lines:

```
BEGIN { m = ARGV[1]; n = ARGV[2]
        for (j = n-m+1; j <= n; j++) {
            t = 1 + int(j * rand())
            if (t in s) s[j] = 1
            else s[t] = 1
        }
        for (i in s) print i
}
```

13.3 Random Permutations

Some programs that use a random sample require that the elements of the sample occur in a random order. Such a sequence is called a random permutation without replacement. In testing a sorting program, for instance, it is important that randomly generated input occur in random order; if the input were always sorted, the test might not fully exercise the sort code.

We could use Floyd's Algorithm F2 to generate a random sample, then copy it to an array, and finally shuffle the elements of the array. This code randomly scrambles the array $X[1..M]$:

```
for I := M downto 2 do
    J := RandInt(1, I)
    Swap(X[J], X[I])
```

This three-step method uses $2M$ calls to RandInt.

After this column originally appeared in *Communications of the ACM*, several readers observed that a slight modification of the above code places a random M-element permutation from the integers in $1..N$ in $X[1..M]$:

```
for I := 1 to N do
    X[I] := I
for I := 1 to M do
    J := RandInt(I, N)
    Swap(X[J], X[I])
```

This algorithm is easy to code, but it requires $O(N)$ run time and $O(N)$ words of memory. Floyd's algorithms, which we'll soon see, are more efficient when N is large compared to M.

Floyd's random permutation generator is similar to his Algorithm F2. To compute an M-element permutation from $1..N$, it first computes an $(M-1)$-element permutation from $1..N-1$. (A recursive version of the algorithm does

not have the variable *J*.) The primary data structure of the permutation generator, though, is a sequence rather than a set. Here is Floyd's Algorithm P:

```
initialize sequence S to empty
for J := N - M + 1 to N do
    T := RandInt(1, J)
    if T is not in S then
        prefix T to S
      else
        insert J in S after T
```

Problem 5 shows that Algorithm P is remarkably efficient in terms of the
number of random bits it uses. Problem 6 deals with efficient implementations
of the sequence *S*.

We can get an intuitive feeling for Algorithm P by considering its behavior
when *M=N*, in which case it generates a random permutation of *N* elements. It
iterates *J* from 1 to *N*. Before execution of the loop body, *S* is a random permutation of the integers in $1..J-1$. The loop body maintains the invariant by
inserting *J* into the sequence; *J* is the first element when *T=J*, otherwise *J* is
placed after one of the $J-1$ existing elements at random.

In general, Algorithm P generates every *M*-element permutation of $1..N$ with
equal probability. Floyd's proof of correctness uses the loop invariant that after
i times through the iteration, $J = N-M+i$ and *S* can be any permutation of *i*
distinct integers in $1..J$, and that there is a single way that the permutation can
be generated.

Doug McIlroy found an elegant way to phrase Floyd's proof: there is one
and only one way to produce each permutation, because the algorithm can be
run backward. Suppose, for instance, that *M=5*, that *N=10*, and that the final
sequence is

    7 2 9 1 5

Because 10 (the final value of *J*) does not occur in *S*, the previous sequence
must have been

    2 9 1 5

and `RandInt` returned *T=7*. Because 9 (the relevant value of *J*) occurs in the
4-element sequence after 2, the previous *T* was 2. Problem 4 shows that one
can similarly recover the entire sequence of random values. Because all random
sequences are supposedly equally likely, all permutations are also.

We can now prove the correctness of Algorithm F2 by its similarity to Algorithm P. At all times, the set *S* in Algorithm F2 contains exactly the elements
in the sequence *S* in Algorithm P. Thus each final *M*-element subset of $1..N$ is
generated by *M*! random sequences, so all occur equiprobably.

13.4 Principles

Algorithm S is a pretty good algorithm, but not good enough for Bob Floyd. Not content with its inefficiency, he developed optimal algorithms for generating random samples and random permutations. His programs are a model of efficiency, simplicity, and elegance. Section 13.6 sketches some of the methods that Floyd uses to achieve such programs.

13.5 Problems

1. How do the various algorithms behave when the `RandInt` procedure is non-random? Consider, for instance, generators that always return 0, or that cycle over a range that is much smaller than or much greater than M or N.

2. Describe efficient representations for the set S in Algorithm F2.

3. Algorithms S and F2 both use a set S. Is a data structure that is efficient in one algorithm necessarily efficient in the other?

4. Complete the proof of correctness of Algorithm P by showing how to compute from a final permutation the sequence of random integer values that produced it.

5. How many random bits does Algorithm P consume? Show that this number is close to optimal. Perform a similar analysis for Algorithm F2. Can you find algorithms that are more efficient?

6. Describe representations for the sequence S such that Algorithm P runs in $O(M)$ expected time or in $O(M \log M)$ worst-case time. Your structures should use $O(M)$ worst-case space.

7. Implement Floyd's algorithms in your favorite programming language.

8. Algorithm F2 is an iterative version of the recursive Algorithm F1. There are many general methods for transforming recursive functions to equivalent iterative programs; one method is often illustrated on a recursive factorial function. Consider a recursive function with this form

```
function A(M)
    if M = 0 then
        return X
    else
        S := A(M-1)
        return G(S, M)
```

where M is an integer, S and X have the same type T, and function G maps a T and an integer to a T. Show how the function can be transformed to this iterative form

```
function B(M)
    S := X
    for J := 1 to M do
        S := G(S, J)
    return S
```

9. Study other algorithms for generating random samples.

13.6 Further Reading

Robert W. Floyd received the ACM Turing Award in 1978. In his Turing lecture on "The Paradigms of Programming", Floyd writes, "In my own experience of designing difficult algorithms, I find a certain technique most helpful in expanding my own capabilities. After solving a challenging problem, I solve it again from scratch, retracing only the *insight* of the earlier solution. I repeat this until the solution is as clear and direct as I can hope for. Then I look for a general rule for attacking similar problems, that *would* have led me to approach the given problem in the most efficient way the first time. Often, such a rule is of permanent value."

Floyd's key rule in this problem was, in his own words, to "look for a mathematical characterization of the solution before you think about an algorithm to obtain it." His key insight dealt with the probability of the algorithm generating any particular subset. When Floyd calculated the probabilities of key events in Algorithm S, he noticed that the denominators were powers of N, while the denominators in the solution were falling factorials. His algorithms use a simple structure to generate the correct probabilities. When Floyd finally conceived Algorithm P, he recalls, "I knew it was right even before I proved it."

Floyd's 1978 Turing lecture was published originally in the August 1979 *Communications of the ACM*. It also appears in the *ACM Turing Award Lectures: The First Twenty Years: 1966–1985*, which was published in 1987 by the ACM Press.

COLUMN 14: **BIRTH OF A CRUNCHER**

Its practitioners give it the glorified name of "numerical analysis", but for most programmers the field of number crunching is a lot like plumbing. We use it often, but we don't think about how it works until something goes wrong.

I once held that Neanderthal view. I was cured by a fine course in numerical analysis, which showed me the elegance of the field. My appraisal of the subject changed from "ugly and useless" to "beautiful and useless". I have good numerical routines available in libraries; why would I ever have to make my own?

I was recently delighted to discover that even for a layman like me, numerical analysis can be useful. This column tells how I used some elementary techniques to write a simple numerical routine. I replaced a library function with a version specialized to the problem at hand. The code grew from five lines to a dozen, but the routine was three times faster and it made a big program run twice as fast.

14.1 The Problem

I was working on a program to compute travelling salesman tours through point sets. A procedure-time profile (as described in Column 1) of the thousand-line program showed that about eighty percent of the time was spent in a five-line routine to compute distances. The specification called for the Euclidean distance between points in K-dimensional space. For instance, the distance between the three-dimensional points (a_1, a_2, a_3) and (b_1, b_2, b_3) is

$$\sqrt{(a_1-b_1)^2 + (a_2-b_2)^2 + (a_3-b_3)^2}$$

Program 1 computes the distance between the points represented by the vectors $A[1..K]$ and $B[1..K]$:

```
Sum := 0.0
for J := 1 to K do
    T := A[J] - B[J]
    Sum := Sum + T*T
return sqrt(Sum)
```

Program 1 has the advantage of simplicity: it is easy to understand. Unfortunately, it has several disadvantages as well. It may, for instance, generate an arithmetic overflow even if all inputs, intermediate differences, and the output are in a valid range. Suppose the machine can represent floating point numbers up to 10^{30} and consider computing the distance between $(0, 0)$ and $(3\times10^{20}, 4\times10^{20})$, which is 5×10^{20}. Squaring the difference $0-3\times10^{20}$ yields 9×10^{40} and an overflow. This problem, and a similar problem with underflow, were not important in the program at hand. The context ensured that differences were neither extremely large nor extremely small.

A second problem with Program 1 is that it is expensive, at least as implemented in C on a VAX-11/750. Section 7.2 sketches the performance of that hardware/software system: arithmetic operations range in cost from 3.3 microseconds for integer addition to 15.7 microseconds for floating-point division. When $K=2$, Program 1 requires a whopping 1140 microseconds to compute the Euclidean distance between a pair of points in the plane. Straightforward experiments (like those described in Section 7.2) showed that the lion's share of that time goes to computing the square root, which requires about 940 microseconds.

My goal for the program was to provide a faster distance routine. Problem 5.4 illustrates a method that works in many applications: we simply remove the sqrt from Program 1. If distances are only compared, then the monotonicity of sqrt makes it superfluous. That wouldn't work on this job — I needed to compare sums of distances. I therefore sought a K-dimensional Euclidean distance routine with the following attributes.

Domain: K is in the range 1..16 (but typically 2, 3 or 4). The coordinates of points are in single-precision.

Accuracy: the single-precision output should be accurate to the last decimal digit, or a relative accuracy of about 10^{-7}.

Robustness: the inputs may be assumed to be well-behaved. Overflow and underflow are not major concerns.

Performance: the routine should be as fast as possible.

The rest of this column will focus on a routine with these characteristics. Problem 17 describes an accurate and robust method that is somewhat slower.

14.2 Newton Iteration

Numerical analysts have developed many techniques for finding a *zero* (or *root*) of a function. Given a function $f(x)$, a zero is a real number r such that $f(r)=0$. To compute $\sqrt{a}$ we can find a zero of $f(x) = x^2-a$; if $r^2-a = 0$, then $r = \sqrt{a}$. Thus if we can find zeroes we can compute square roots.

So how do we find the zero of a function? We could use our old friend, binary search. If $a\geqslant1$, then $\sqrt{a}$ is in the range $[1,a]$. We can successively halve that range until we get a good approximation to $\sqrt{a}$. If $a=4$, for instance, we will examine the ranges [1,4], [1,2.5], [1.75,2.5], [1.75,2.125], ... Numerical analysts call this the *bisection* method; each step yields one additional bit of accuracy in the answer.

A superior scheme was invented by Isaac Newton, an English computer scientist who also dabbled in mathematics and physics. His method does not compute a range explicitly, but rather starts with an initial guess x_0 and generates a sequence of approximations x_1, x_2, x_3, ... To generate x_{i+1} we must know both $f(x_i)$ and its derivative $f'(x_i)$. We then proceed down the tangent line until it crosses the x-axis:

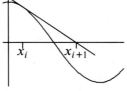

Intuitively, we are approximating the function locally by a straight line with equal y-value and slope. Mathematically, we compute the next iteration by

$$x_{i+1} = x_i - f(x_i)/f'(x_i)$$

To use Newton iteration we must therefore be able to compute both the function and its derivative.

To find $\sqrt{a}$ we will find the zero of $f(x) = x^2 - a$, so $f'(x) = 2x$. Newton's iteration formula is then

$$x_{i+1} = x_i - (x_i^2 - a)/2x_i$$

$$= x_i - x_i/2 + a/2x_i$$

$$= (x_i + a/x_i)/2$$

For an intuitive appreciation of why the formula works, observe that if x_i is too small then a/x_i is too big; the average of the two is a better estimate. (School children call this the "divide and average" technique.) Thus once we reach the final answer, we don't move away: if $x_i = \sqrt{a}$, then

$$x_{i+1} = (\sqrt{a} + a/\sqrt{a})/2 = \sqrt{a}$$

Here is a graphical representation of one step of Newton iteration for finding $\sqrt{2}$, in which $a=2$, $x_0=2$, and $x_1 = (2+2/2)/2 = 1.5$:

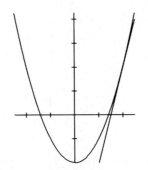

The figure hints at the rapid rate at which this method converges, but the story can't be told graphically. Here are the next few elements in the sequence x_i:

```
2.0000000000000000
1.5000000000000000
1.4166666666666667
1.4142156862745098
1.4142135623746899
1.4142135623730951
```

The values were computed by the simple "scaffolding" program shown in Solution 6. The final answer is correct to 16 decimal places.

14.3 A Great Place to Start

There's the basic idea of Newton iteration. Two problems stand between us and a program:

What is a good initial value x_0?

How many iterations should be made until an iteration x_i is declared to be the final answer?

We will explore the second question in the next section; this section concentrates on the first.

The example in the previous section showed Newton's method converging quickly. Each iteration roughly doubled the number of accurate digits. Because the error at the $i+1^{st}$ step is proportional to the square of the error at the ith step, numerical analysts refer to this as "quadratic convergence". That behavior is typical of the method, so long as two conditions hold. The first requirement is that the derivative is not near zero. That is always true for square roots, so long as we compute $\sqrt{0}$ as a special case, but it can be difficult for other functions.

The second requirement for quadratic convergence is that the initial guess must be near enough to the final root. When the current value is far from the square root, Newton's method gives only one bit of accuracy per iteration. Here is the convergence to $\sqrt{2}$, starting from 1000:

```
1000.0000000000000000
 500.0010000000000000
 250.0024999960000100
 125.0052499580004700
  62.5106246430170320
  31.2713096020621940
  15.6676329948683660
   7.8976423478563581
   4.0754412405194990
   2.2830928243925538
   1.5795487524060154
   1.4228665795786682
   1.4142398735915306
   1.4142135626178485
   1.4142135623730951
```

Beware, though, that for functions less well behaved, Newton's method will not even converge if it starts far from the root.

Most general-purpose square root routines get an initial guess by black magic of some sort, such as extracting the bit field that is the exponent of a floating point number and halving it to approximate the square root. (Using the last square root computed is effective in some applications; see Problem 9.) In the context of a distance function, we can use other information to get the initial guess. When K is 2, for instance, we wish to compute $a=\sqrt{b^2+c^2}$:

We can use the maximum of b and c (b in the above figure) as the initial guess x_0. Thus we have the inequalities

$$c \leqslant b \leqslant a = \sqrt{b^2+c^2} \leqslant \sqrt{2 \times b^2} = \sqrt{2} \times b$$

so we know that a is in the range $[b, \sqrt{2} \times b]$.

In higher dimensions we will use as an initial estimate the maximum of the differences in all dimensions, which we'll call D. The distance is at least D and the sum of the squares of the K differences is at most $K \times D^2$, so the distance is in the range $[D, D\sqrt{K}]$.

14.4 The Code

We can now write a program for computing Euclidean distances. It uses as its initial value the maximum difference, and iterates until two subsequent values are reasonably close: until $|x_{i+1}-x_i|/x_{i+1}$ is at most one part in ten

million, which corresponds to single-precision accuracy on my machine. Here is
Program 2:

```
T := abs(A[1] - B[1])
Max := T; Sum := T*T
for J := 2 to K do
    T := abs(A[J] - B[J])
    if T > Max then Max := T
    Sum := Sum + T*T
if Sum = 0.0 then return 0.0
/* find sqrt(Sum), starting at Max */
Eps = 1.0e-7
Z := Max
loop
    NewZ := 0.5 * (Z + Sum/Z)
    if abs(NewZ-Z) <= Eps*NewZ then break
    Z := NewZ
return NewZ
```

A table at the end of this section displays the run time of all programs discussed in this column. The table shows that Program 2 is about 35% faster
than Program 1 when $K=2$: the new square root code is indeed faster than the
system routine. When $K=16$, though, Program 2 is only about 1.5% faster than
Program 1: the bottleneck in this case is not the square root, and finding the
maximum difference chews up most of the time saved by the faster root-finder.
Fortunately, the specifications stated that K tends to be small.

There are two ways to improve Program 2. We'll start by speeding up the
root-finder, and then shortly work on computing the maximum difference. The
current version iterates until it is close enough; the next version will iterate a
fixed number of times guaranteed to produce convergence. That will remove the
cost of loop overhead, of testing for convergence, and of computing the final
iteration that is so close to its predecessor.

So how many iterations do we need? The specifications state that $K \leqslant 16$
and that we must compute to single-precision accuracy. Because $K \leqslant 16$, we
know that the distance is at most $\sqrt{16} \times D$ (where D is the maximum difference,
max), and therefore in the range $[D, 4D]$. It seemed that the geometric mean
of that range, $2D$, would make a good initial value. I used my scaffolding program to examine the convergence from that midpoint to the bounds of the
range. I first computed $\sqrt{1}$ starting from 2:

```
        x                 abs(x-1.0)/1.0
2.0000000000000000    1.0000000000000000
1.2500000000000000    0.2500000000000000
1.0250000000000000    0.0250000000000000
1.0003048780487805    0.0003048780487805
1.0000000464611473    0.0000000464611473
1.0000000000000011    0.0000000000000011
1.0000000000000000    0.0000000000000000
```

In the next experiment I used the scaffolding program to compute $\sqrt{16}$ from the same starting value of 2:

```
        x                        abs(x-4.0)/4.0
2.000000000000000          0.5000000000000000
5.000000000000000          0.2500000000000000
4.100000000000000          0.0250000000000000
4.0012195121951220         0.0003048780487805
4.0000001858445894         0.0000000464611473
4.0000000000000043         0.0000000000000011
4.0000000000000000         0.0000000000000000
```

Because Newton iteration scales linearly, these two cases model computing $\sqrt{D^2}$ and $\sqrt{16D^2}$ from any starting value $2D$. Problem 15 proves that these two extremes are indeed the two that are slowest to converge. The right columns show that after the first step the two inputs give the same relative error. The process yields the required seven-digit accuracy after four steps. A loop unrolled four times thus computes an accurate answer when $K \leqslant 16$. The first part of Program 3 is the same as Program 2. Here are the final lines of Program 3:

```
    ... same as Program 2 ...
/* compute sqrt(Sum), starting at 2.0*Max */
Max := Max * 2.0
Max := 0.5 * (Max + Sum/Max)
Max := 0.5 * (Max + Sum/Max)
Max := 0.5 * (Max + Sum/Max)
return 0.5 * (Max + Sum/Max)
```

This program is about twice as fast as Program 2 when $K=4$. Problem 11 suggests a further speedup to computing square roots: use table lookup to obtain a better initial guess. The above numerical examples show that if we can get the relative error down to 2.5%, then two further iterations suffice for single-precision accuracy.

The final improvements leave the lofty planes of numerical analysis to employ a couple of old coding tricks. The first one is specialized to the C language. Both the real program and the test program implemented a vector of points as a two-dimensional array of floating point numbers. The final program introduced two new variables to point to the two Euclidean points being compared, and thus replaced K two-dimensional array accesses with K references to a one-dimensional vector. The second trick is described in Problem 10; it exploits an algebraic identity. Because these speedups are quite particular to the implementation language, Program 4 was timed but it is not shown in a pseudocode version.

The routines are summarized in the table below. The speedup from Program 1 to Program 4 is a factor of 3.5 for $K=2$, 2.8 for $K=4$, and 1.9 for $K=16$.

PROGRAM NUMBER	MICROSECONDS		
	K = 2	K = 4	K = 16
1	1140	1270	2030
2	730	990	2000
3	350	500	1340
4	330	450	1070

14.5 Principles

Distance computations are the workhorse in many programs. The new distance routine doubled the speed of my 1000-line travelling salesman program, and similar speedups are common for other geometric programs. Besides producing a useful routine, this exercise has illustrated several general principles.

The Importance of Context. The process of producing a fast distance routine changes dramatically with many factors. For instance, most of the work described in this column would have been counterproductive on a system with a hardware square root instruction. For large values of K (say, 1000), the cost of the square root is relatively minor. For $K=2$ (that is, for planar points), the method sketched in Problem 17 is often faster than Program 4 and always more robust. One must know a great deal of context before starting to code.

Newton Iteration. This technique is often used by numerical analysts, and is sometimes useful even to mere mortal programmers — see Problem 1.

Coding Tricks. Though the big improvements are usually due to algorithmic changes, little improvements to code can reduce run time. In this case study, unrolling the iteration loop was effective: it removes loop overhead, convergence testing, and an extra iteration. Other tricks include exploiting algebraic identities, optimizing array references, and storing precomputed answers in tables (see Problems 10, 11 and 12).

The Role of Libraries. An excellent library is a delight to use. Many libraries provide accurate and numerically robust code. It is wise to remember, though, that few routines can be all things to all users. In this case, special-purpose code was tailored to the context in which it was used to be more efficient than the general routine. Re-usability and numerical accuracy were sacrificed for speed. In this case, that was a sound engineering tradeoff.

14.6 Problems

1. Your library square root routine provides only single-precision accuracy, yet your application requires double precision. What do you do?

2. On a hand-held calculator, repeatedly take the square root of a number then square it back again. What does this tell you about the calculator?

3. Newton's method does not work when $f'(x)=0$. This happens for square roots when computing $\sqrt{0}$. How does Newton's method attempt to compute $\sqrt{0}$ from a starting value of $x_0=1$? Does the algorithm have similar problems for computing the root of a positive number near zero?

4. Study the square root routine provided by your system. If it uses Newton's method, what is its initial value and how many iterations does it make?

5. Some computers have fast hardware multipliers and no hardware dividers. They implement division by multiplying by an inverse. Show how to compute $1/a$ by using Newton's method to find a zero of the function $f(x) = a-1/x$. Try using Newton's method to compute cube roots, or to find roots of arbitrary polynomials.

6. Implement a "scaffolding" program for Newton iteration. Its input is a number whose square root is to be taken, a starting value, and the number of iterations to be performed; provide defaults. Its output is a trace of the values and the relative errors.

7. Implement Programs 1, 2, 3 and 4 on your system. How do you test their correctness? Build a testbed for timing them. How do your results compare to the times presented in this column?

8. [J. L. Blue] This column explicitly ignored the problems of overflow and underflow in summing the squares of differences. Write a program that is sensitive to those problems.

9. A common heuristic uses the last square root computed as the starting value for the next Newton iteration. Measure this in an application. How many iterations does it make on the average? How does it compare to other starting values?

10. Program 3 doubles Max only to halve it in the next statement; use algebraic identities to speed up those statements:

```
Max := Max * 2.0
Max := 0.5 * (Max + 0.mm/Max)
```

11. Table lookup can speed up a program by trading space for run time. How can this technique be used in computing a good starting value? How could you use table lookup to compute Euclidean distances if the planar point set has both x and y coordinates in the range 0..9999?

12. [A. Appel] Show how the K absolute values used by Program 2 to compute Max can be replaced with a single absolute value. (Hint: keep track of the largest square seen so far.)

13. Hardware designers have observed that a division and a square root box of comparable efficiency require comparable amounts of hardware. Show that square root is about as hard as division in software, too, by sketching a routine to compute $\sqrt{2}$ accurate to one million decimal digits.

14. [S. Crocker] Consideration of finite-precision arithmetic complicates many programs, but makes this square root routine particularly simple:

```
X := 1
loop
    NewX := 0.5 * (X + A/X)
    if NewX = X then return NewX
    X := NewX
```

Does it converge on your machine for all nonzero inputs A? On all machines? (For a better starting value, see Problem 9.)

15. [M. D. McIlroy] What is the best starting value for Newton's method for square roots in a bounded range? Let n be a natural number and let a, b and r be reals satisfying $0 < a \leqslant r \leqslant b$; let $R = r^2$. Given n, a, and b, we desire to choose a starting value $x_0 = x$ for the Newton iteration $x_{i+1} = (x_i + R/x_i)/2$ to minimize the worst-case relative error

$$max_{a \leqslant r \leqslant b} \ |x_n - r| /r$$

Show that the optimal choice is $x_0 = \sqrt{ab}$, independent of the value of n.

16. Problem 15 identifies the best starting value for Newton iteration. How many iterations are required as a function of the number of dimensions (K) and the desired accuracy?

17. Moler and Morrison have described a fast, robust and portable algorithm for computing $\sqrt{P^2 + Q^2}$ (see "Replacing Square Roots by Pythagorean Sums" in the *IBM Journal of Research and Development 27*, 6, pp. 577–581, November 1983). Their algorithm can be sketched as

```
P := abs(P); Q := abs(Q)
if P < Q then Swap(P, Q)
if P = 0.0 then return Q
repeat IterCount times
    R := Q / P
    R := R * R
    R := R / (4 + R)
    P := P + 2*R*P
    Q := Q * R
return P
```

Its cubic convergence means that the result is accurate to 6.5 decimal digits after two iterations, to 20 digits after three iterations, and to 62 digits after four iterations. Its intermediate results avoid overflow and underflow.

a. Use this code in a subroutine to compute planar Euclidean distances. How does its run time compare to Program 3 when $K=2$?

b. How can you use this routine to compute Euclidean distances in K space? How long would your code take when $K=1000$, and how does that compare to Program 3?

18. How would you write a Euclidean distance routine to run on a parallel processor that can perform P arithmetic operations at once?

14.7 Further Reading

There are dozens of excellent textbooks on numerical analysis. Which one is best for you depends on your desires for breadth and depth and your interest in mathematics and code.

14.8 A Big Success Story *[Sidebar]*

The body of this column describes a few hours' work by an amateur, using techniques ranging in age from a few decades to a few centuries. We'll now turn to a numerical success story on a grander scale. Everyone knows of the tremendous advances made in computer hardware over the last few decades. This section will show how numerical analysis has kept squarely up with that brisk pace (but with less fanfare in the popular press).

In Section 10.3.C of his *Numerical Methods, Software, and Analysis* (published in 1983 by McGraw-Hill), John Rice chronicles the algorithmic history of three-dimensional elliptic partial differential equations. Such problems arise in simulations as diverse as VLSI devices, oil wells, nuclear reactors, and airfoils. A small part of that history (mostly but not entirely from Rice's book) is given in the following table. The run time gives the number of floating point operations required to solve the problem on an $N \times N \times N$ grid.

Method	Year	Run Time
Gaussian Elimination	1945	N^7
SOR Iteration (Suboptimal Parameters)	1954	$8N^5$
SOR Iteration (Optimal Parameters)	1960	$8N^4 \log N$
Cyclic Reduction	1970	$8N^3 \log N$
Multigrid	1978	$60N^3$

SOR stands for "successive over-relaxation". The $O(N^3)$ running time of the Multigrid algorithm is within a constant factor of optimal because the problem has that many inputs. Even using the 1970 algorithm, the time required to compute the solution is usually less than the time to read the inputs. Subsequent research on the problem has therefore concentrated on numerically robust solutions to ill-behaved equations.

Computing hardware has also seen dramatic improvements. This table describes several supercomputers that were the most powerful computing engines of their time.

Machine	Year Delivered	Megaflops
Manchester Mark I	1947	0.0002
IBM 701	1954	0.003
IBM Stretch	1960	0.3
CDC 6600	1964	2
CDC 7600	1969	5
Cray-1	1976	50
Cray-2 (Estimated; One CPU)	1985	125

The performance is measured in million of floating point operations per second. I've tried to factor in the "overhead" instructions that accompany the "real" floating-point operations. Although any such table is necessarily suspect, I think that no entry in the above table is off by much more than a factor of two.

To compare the hardware and software speedups, let's consider solving a smooth problem, Poisson's equation, using $N=64$. The bottom curve in the following graph illustrates hardware improvements by running the 1945 algorithm on various hardware, and the middle curve runs the various algorithms on the 1947 hardware. The top curve shows the combined speedup.

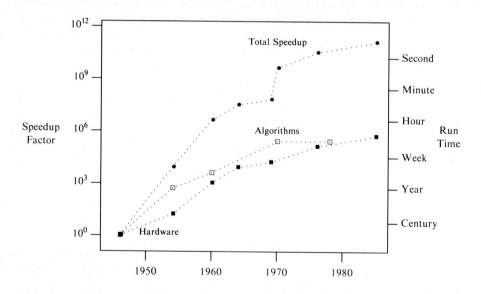

The algorithmic speedup is a factor of a quarter million over a period of thirty years, and the hardware speedup is half a million over forty years. Each speedup by itself reduces the run time from centuries to hours. Together, they multiply to reduce the run time to less than a second.

COLUMN 15: **SELECTION**

Suppose you have a list of heights of 101 people. It isn't too hard to find the tallest or the shortest on the list, but how would you identify the most mediocre person (speaking only heightwise, of course)? That is, how would you find the person on the list who is taller than the fifty shortest people and shorter than the fifty tallest?

The next section describes the problem around which this column is built: selecting the Kth-smallest member in a set of N elements. A program for the task is derived in the following section, and the subsequent section analyzes its rapid running time.

15.1 The Problem

This excerpt from a table entitled "Density of Population by States" gives the 1980 figures in persons per square mile.

Name	Population Density
West Virginia	80.8
North Carolina	120.4
Virginia	134.7
Pennsylvania	264.3
New York	370.6
Maryland	428.7
Connecticut	637.8
New Jersey	986.2
District of Columbia	10,132.3

If you had to choose a single number to characterize the "typical" density in these nine contiguous areas, what would it be? The average or arithmetic mean value is 1461.8, but that seems too high: it is greater than eight of the nine

159

values. New York's "middle" value of 370.6 seems more representative; it is the fifth largest of the nine. Statisticians refer to the $M+1^{st}$-smallest element in a set of $2M+1$ elements as the *median*, or its 50th percentile. We'll use medians and other percentiles later in this column to analyze data on the run time of the selection algorithm.

Computer scientists use medians in many "divide-and-conquer" algorithms. The median partitions a set into two subsets which an algorithm then processes recursively; Problem 8 uses an algorithm with this structure. Furthermore, the selection problem is a practical introduction to the theoretical field of comparison algorithms; Problem 9 presents two other representative problems.

Let's turn now from the abstract world of sets to the concrete world of programs. The input to our selection routine will be the positive integer N, the array $X[1..N]$, and the positive integer $K \leqslant N$. The program must permute the array so that $X[1..K-1] \leqslant X[K] \leqslant X[K+1..N]$. At that point, the Kth-smallest element in the set resides in its proper position, $X[K]$.

15.2 The Program

A simple selection program merely sorts the array X. Unfortunately, this straightforward solution requires $O(N \log N)$ time. In this section we'll study a faster algorithm due to C. A. R. Hoare. His method selects the Kth-smallest element in just $O(N)$ average time. Hoare called his program *Find*; I'll refer to the implementation in this column as *Select*.

Hoare's selection algorithm is closely related to his Quicksort program. That divide-and-conquer algorithm can be sketched as

```
procedure QSort(set S): sequence
   if size(S) <= 1 then
      return the element in S
   else
      partition S around a random element
         T into subsets A and B such that
         elements in A are less than T and
         elements in B are greater than T
      return QSort(A) followed by T
         followed by QSort(B)
```

The procedure's input is a set and its output is the sequence of elements in sorted order. Both input and output structures can be efficiently implemented in a single array: the sequence in the subvector $X[L..U]$ is represented by the two integers L and U.

The Select algorithm has the same structure as Quicksort. Given $L \leqslant K \leqslant U$, its first step in finding the proper occupant of $X[K]$ is to partition the array around a random element. While Quicksort then recursively operates on both subsequences, Select saves time by recurring only on the side that contains K. Here is Select as it finds the median of a 21-element array:

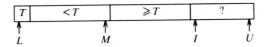

Each level in the picture represents a stage of the algorithm, and the array's final configuration is described in the last level. The partitioning element is circled. Elements to its left have lesser values, while elements to its right are greater than or equal to the partitioning value.

An iterative selection algorithm can be sketched as follows.

```
set range to entire array
while range is large do
      partition range
      repeat on proper subrange
```

We'll first study the partitioning code, and then turn to the complete algorithm.

The routine partitions the array $X[L..U]$ around the value $T=X[L]$. After the $I-1^{st}$ step of the iteration, the loop invariant is depicted as

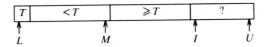

The iterative step inspects the Ith element. If $X[I] \geqslant T$ then the invariant remains true. When $X[I]<T$, we regain the invariant by incrementing M to index the new location of the small element, and then swapping $X[M]$ with $X[I]$. The loop terminates with $I=U+1$, leaving

We then swap $X[L]$ with $X[M]$ to give

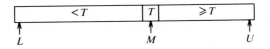

That final swap ensures that we can operate next on $L..M-1$ or $M+1..U$. In both cases, we exclude $X[M]$, and thereby avoid an infinite loop.

Partitioning around the first element in the array can require excessive time for some common inputs — for instance, arrays that are already sorted. We do better to choose a partitioning element at random. We'll accomplish this by swapping $X[L]$ with a random entry in $X[L..U]$, using the function RandInt(L,U) described in Section 13.1 which returns a random integer in the range $L..U$. The complete partitioning code is

```
Swap(X[L], X[RandInt(L,U)])
M := L
for I := L+1 to U do
    if X[I] < X[L] then
        M := M+1
        Swap(X[M], X[I])
Swap(X[L], X[M])
```

Upon termination, we know that $X[L..M-1] < X[M] \leqslant X[M+1..U]$.

With this partitioning code in hand, we can turn our attention to the complete selection subroutine. Our first version is recursive: *Select* (L, U, K) partitions the array $X[L..U]$ so that $X[L..K-1] \leqslant X[K] \leqslant X[K+1..U]$. If $L \geqslant U$ then the subarray contains at most one element, so we can halt. Otherwise, we partition the array around the element T, which is placed in $X[M]$. The position of K relative to M gives three cases:

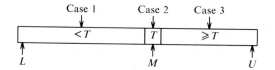

Case 2 is the easiest. When $K=M$, the Kth-smallest element is in its final place and the program is finished. When $K<M$ we have Case 1: the Kth-smallest element can't be in $X[M..U]$, so we exclude that range by recursively operating on the range $L..M-1$. Case 3 is similar, and the recursive routine can be sketched as

```
procedure Select(L, U, K)
    pre L <= K <= U
    post X[L..K-1] <= X[K] <= X[K+1..U]
if L < U then
    /* Partition X[L..U] so that
        X[L..M-1] <= X[M] <= X[M+1..U] */
    if      K < M then Select(L, M-1, K)
    else if K > M then Select(M+1, U, K)
    /* else K = M so finished */
```

Since $X[M]$ is excluded by each recursive call, the program can't have an infinite loop.

The recursive calls in the above procedure are of a special form called *tail recursion*: the call is always the last action in a procedure. A tail-recursive procedure can always be transformed into an equivalent procedure with a while loop. We'll now study an iterative selection subroutine, which we saw earlier in Section 3.2. It uses L and U as local variables, maintaining the relation that $L \leqslant K \leqslant U$ until the final step. After partitioning around $X[M]$, the code adjusts L or U (and sometimes both) to narrow the range $L..U$. Here is the final version of the Select program:

```
procedure Select(K)
      pre:   1 <= K <= N
      post: X[1..K-1] <= X[K] <= X[K+1..N]
   L := 1; U := N
   while L < U do
          /* Invariant: X[1..L-1] <= X[L..U] <= X[U+1..N] */
          Swap(X[L], X[RandInt(L,U)])
          M := L
          for I := L+1 to U do
              /* Invariant: X[L+1..M]   <   X[L]
                        and X[M+1..I-1] >= X[L] */
              if X[I] < X[L] then
                  M := M+1
                  Swap(X[M], X[I])
          Swap(X[L], X[M])
          /* X[1..L-1] <= X[L..U] <= X[U+1..N]
             and X[L..M-1] < X[M] <= X[M+1..U] */
          if K <= M then U := M-1
          if K >= M then L := M+1
```

This is the Select algorithm we'll study in the rest of this column, and it is fine for typical day-to-day use. There are, however, several improvements that one should incorporate into an industrial-strength selection routine. Speedups to the partitioning code are described in Problems 1, 2, 4 and 5.

15.3 Analysis of Run Time

In the previous section we derived a selection routine and informally analyzed its correctness: it halts on all inputs, and always computes the correct answer. We'll turn now to its allegedly linear run time. The intuitive idea behind the $O(N)$ average time is that typical iterations remove a substantial fraction of the range $L..U$. If each step were to remove half the elements, then an identity like

$$N + N/2 + N/4 + N/8 + \cdots \leqslant 2N$$

would describe the total run time.

This section supports our intuition with observations of the algorithm at work. In addition to insight about Select, this exercise illustrates general techniques for the empirical analysis of algorithms. (Problem 6 introduces the mathematical analysis of selection algorithms.)

The first figure in Section 15.2 illustrates the algorithm's behavior on an array of 21 elements. That figure is useful as one first studies the algorithm, but it is too detailed to give much insight into the algorithm's performance. Here is a similar picture of an array, and a "stick diagram" representation of the same computation:

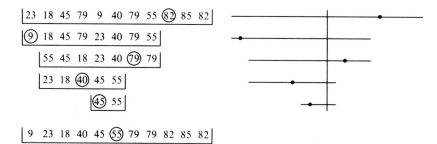

```
 23 18 45 79  9 40 79 55 ⑧② 85 82

 ⑨ 18 45 79 23 40 79 55

    55 45 18 23 40 ⑦⑨ 79

    23 18 ④⓪ 45 55

          ④⑤ 55

 9  23 18 40 45 ⑤⑤ 79 79 82 85 82
```

The horizontal lines represent the subrange $L..U$ at each iteration, the bullets represent the partitioning elements, and the vertical line represents K. The stick diagram contains less information than the array (we don't know the values being permuted), but it shows the key issue in performance: the size of the subarrays throughout the computation.

I generated the figure by adding print statements at key positions in a selection routine. The resulting output was processed by a program written in the Grap language for describing graphical displays of data. The array portion of the figure requires the complete information. The stick diagram, on the other hand, can be constructed by this program that stores only the values of L and U, and does away entirely with the array X:

```
L := 1; U := N
while L < U do
    decrement Y
    M := RandInt(L, U)
    draw a line from L, Y to U, Y
    plot a bullet at M, Y
    if K <= M then U := M-1
    if K >= M then L := M+1
```

If the array contains no duplicate elements, then randomly choosing the partition element makes it equally likely to wind up in every position between L and U. For that reason, the above code sets M to a random integer in that range. The statistical nature of the algorithm's performance makes no assumption about the probability distribution of the inputs; the variation is a function of the randomizing *Swap* statement. Here are five runs of the program to select the median of 101 elements. The integer plotted at the right of each run is the total number of comparisons used by the process.

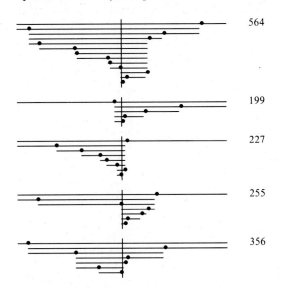

564

199

227

255

356

The model of each step halving the range implies that selecting the median of 101 elements requires roughly

$$100 + 50 + 25 + \cdots = 200$$

comparisons. The above figure shows that the model is imperfect yet still useful. The second computation was quite close to the model: each guess came close to halving the existing interval. The first computation was particularly unlucky; it chose several partitioning elements near the end of the range. The next three runs fall between those two extremes. The halving model suggests that the algorithm uses $2N$ comparisons. These experiments suggest that the program runs in $C_{median} \cdot N$ comparisons for some value of $C_{median} \approx ?$

To estimate the constant C_{median}, we'll gather data on the number of comparisons used by the algorithm. Instead of running the complete algorithm on real data, we'll use this "skeleton" program to count comparisons.

```
CCount := 0
L := 1; U := N
while L < U do
     CCount := CCount + U-L
     M := RandInt(L, U)
     if K <= M then U := M-1
     if K >= M then L := M+1
```

The Select program uses $U-L$ comparisons to partition the $U-L+1$ elements in the range $L..U$. The above program can simulate the computation on a set of size $N=10^6$ in a few dozen steps rather than a few million steps.

The next figure plots the results of selecting the median 101 times at five different values of N, ranging from 101 to 1,000,001. The left graph presents the complete data: each mark records the number of comparisons in one experiment divided by N, which estimates the constant C_{median}. Thus C_{median} appears to be between 2 and 6, but the sheer bulk of the data hides the information.

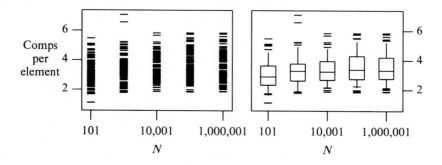

The right graph summarizes the left graph using J. W. Tukey's "box-and-whiskers plots". The middle horizontal line in the box denotes the median of the samples, and the top and bottom lines denote the upper and lower quartiles (in this case, the 26th- and 76th-smallest elements in the set of 101 real numbers). The lines out of the box show the spread to the 5th and 95th percentiles, and the extreme points beyond those percentiles are plotted explicitly. By highlighting the important quantiles, the box plot shows that C_{median} tends to be between 3 and 4. In 1971, Knuth showed mathematically that its average value tends to 3.39 as N grows large. The five medians in the right graph are, in increasing order, 2.90, 3.28, 3.24, 3.37, and 3.32.

So far we have concentrated on computing the median. The next graph presents data on selecting the Kth value, for $K = 1, 100,001, 200,001, ...,$ 1,000,001 and N fixed at 1,000,001. It suggests that the median is the most expensive to compute, while other values tend to require fewer computations.

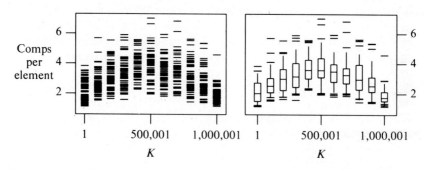

The box-and-whiskers plot in the right graph presents the information more clearly. We already knew that the median requires about $3.4N$ comparisons. This graph suggests that the minimum and maximum require about $2N$

comparisons. It also suggests that the cost is symmetric around the median. This makes sense intuitively — selecting the Kth-smallest is just selecting the $(N-K)^{th}$-largest with the comparisons reversed.

So far our analysis of Select has concentrated on the fact that it uses $O(N)$ comparisons. Because it does only some constant number of other operations along with each comparison, its total running time is also linear. To gain further insight I implemented Select in C on a VAX-11/750 and compared it to the C library subroutine qsort. The system sort required about $100N \log_2 N$ microseconds to sort an array of N elements, while Select found the median in about $100N$ microseconds. For $N=100,000$, this translates into ten seconds for Select versus almost three minutes for the sort.

15.4 Principles

We have analyzed two aspects of Hoare's selection algorithm: its answer is *correct*, and it computes that answer *efficiently*. This exercise illustrates two important points about the analysis of programs.

A Spectrum of Analyses. There are several reasons why I believe that the Select program is correct. This column presented both an informal correctness argument and pictures showing the algorithm at work (generated by the program itself). Section 3.2 describes scaffolding for viewing the program at work and for testing the program. Each of these analyses supports the others: watching the program at work gives insight into its loop invariant, which in turn is useful for testing.

I am also convinced that Select runs in $O(N)$ time on arrays with few duplicated elements. This column supports that premise with an informal mathematical argument (the "halving model") and a series of experiments observing the program at work. The experiments progressed from detailed pictures of the array to "stick diagrams" illustrating the size of the subrange to graphs counting the number of comparisons. Each experiment in the series described more computations but gave less information about each one. Problem 6 continues this trend, and shows how abstraction of the program can eventually lead to a mathematical analysis.

Skeleton Programs. We saw several programs that provide information about Select without performing all the work of the complete program. Problem 6 describes several additional programs with this flavor. While Select would use several billion steps on a set of size one billion, these programs can gather information on the same computation in just a few dozen operations. These programs represent important midpoints on the spectrum of analyses sketched above.

Graphical Methods in Analysis. Graphical output is now available to many programmers; we should use it to understand our programs. All pictures in this column were drawn by simple programs (between ten and thirty lines of code). We understood the correctness of the algorithm with detailed pictures showing the history of the computations and "array boxes" that illustrated the loop invariants. Graphical displays allow us to analyze a large volume of experimental data. The right graph in the last figure, for instance, uses about 150 horizontal and vertical line segments to represent 550 computations that together represent over a billion comparisons. The mathematical analysis of most algorithms is downright hard, but simulations and pictures are well within the grasp of most programmers.

15.5 Problems

1. Select partitions about a random element in the subrange. Study the effectiveness of using other partitioning elements (such as the median of the first, middle and last elements in the array or an appropriate representative of a larger sample).

2. The Select algorithm and its derivatives aren't always the best ways to implement selection. How would you select the second-smallest element in a three-element array? What if $K=6$ and $N=11$? What if $K=1000$ and the $N=1,000,000$ input values were stored on a reel of magnetic tape?

3. How would you find the median of one million values stored on magnetic tape if your computer had only one tape drive and about a dozen words of main memory? How would you use a second tape drive?

4. Although Select runs in $O(N)$ average time, it requires $O(N^2)$ time in the worst case. Describe a selection algorithm with $O(N)$ worst-case time.

5. Perform experiments and display data for the following problems.

    a. The discussion of run time concentrated on the number of comparisons used; that is a good but sometimes imperfect indicator of cost on a real machine. Implement a selection algorithm and measure its run time. Any surprises?

    b. Delete the randomizing Swap statement from the Select program. How does the average run time change? Describe an input that achieves the worst possible run time.

    c. The first graph in Section 15.3 held K fixed at $(N+1)/2$ and varied N, and the next graph held N fixed at 1,000,001 and varied K. Describe the function of two variables that tells the average number of comparisons needed to find the Kth-smallest element in a set of N distinct elements. In particular, what is the shape of the curve induced by varying K when N is fixed? When K is fixed at a constant fraction of N, how does that curve behave?

    d. Our analyses assumed that the input array contained no duplicated elements. How does Select perform if some array elements appear many times? How can that performance be improved?

6. This problem mathematically investigates the performance of Select when it is called with $K=1$, that is, when it selects the least element in the array. The skeleton program that counts comparisons (without actually selecting the least element) simplifies to

```
U := N
while U > 1 do
    CCount := CCount + U-1
    U := RandInt(1,U) - 1
```

Show that this recursive program computes the same function

```
function CCount(N)
    if N <= 1 then
        return 0
    else
        return N-1 + CCount(RandInt(0,N-1))
```

If C_N denotes the average value of *CCount* (N) after the code is executed, show that it satisfies the recurrence relation

$$C_0 = C_1 = 0$$

$$C_N = N-1 + 1/N \sum_{0 \leqslant i \leqslant N-1} C_i$$

Write a program that computes $C_0, C_1, ..., C_M$. (Hint: first use a table $C[0..M]$ and $O(M^2)$ time, then make your algorithm run in $O(M)$ time, and finally remove the table.) Use that program to characterize the behavior of C_N. One possible use is to run the program to gather data, while another approach studies its structure to see how to "telescope" the recurrence analytically.

7. [J. M. Chambers] The Select algorithm ensures that for a single value of K, $X[1..K-1] \leqslant X[K] \leqslant X[K+1..N]$, while Quicksort establishes that condition for all values of K. The problem of "Partial Sorting" calls for establishing the condition for a set of integers in the range $1..N$. For instance, in drawing box plots of 101 values we were interested in the set $\{6, 26, 51, 76, 96\}$. Show how to modify the Quicksort/Select idea to compute partial sorts. Given the input arrays $1 \leqslant K[1] \leqslant K[2] \leqslant \cdots \leqslant K[M] \leqslant N$ and $X[1..N]$, the program should establish

$$X[1..K[1]-1] \leqslant X[K[1]] \leqslant$$

$$X[K[1]+1..K[2]-1] \leqslant X[K[2]] \leqslant$$

$$X[K[2]+1..K[3]-1] \leqslant X[K[3]] \leqslant \cdots$$

8. For this problem, assume that every element of the array X has two fields: $X[I].key$ is the key of the Ith element, and $X[I].wt$ is its weight (a positive real number). Let S denote $\sum_{1 \leqslant i \leqslant N} X[i].wt$. The "weighted median"

problem calls for computing the integer K and partitioning the array such that these conditions hold:

$$X[1..K-1].key \leqslant X[K].key \leqslant X[K+1..N].key$$

$$\sum_{1 \leqslant i < K} X[i].wt < S/2$$

$$\sum_{K < i \leqslant N} X[i].wt < S/2$$

Modify Select to perform this task in linear expected time. Show how to use a solution to Problem 4 as a subroutine to solve this problem in linear worst-case time. Modify both algorithms to find other "weighted quantiles": given a real $0 < Q < 1$, find a record such that the weights of lesser keys sum to at most QS, while the weights of greater keys sum to at most $(1-Q)S$.

9.   Give algorithms for finding both the minimum and maximum elements in a set and for finding the maximum and second-largest elements. Try to use as few comparisons as possible.

10. Experiment with other graphical representations of computations. This picture, for instance, illustrates the computation depicted in the final figure in Section 15.2. Numbers in that figure are represented here as vertical bars. Try "animating" such a representation in a simple movie.

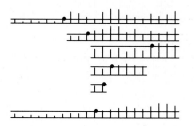

15.6 Further Reading

Hoare originally described Quicksort and Find in one page of the July 1961 *Communications of the ACM*. He illustrated the young field of program verification by arguing the correctness of Find in the January 1971 *Communications*. Knuth analyzed the run time of the algorithm in his "Mathematical Analysis of Algorithms" on pages 19–27 of the proceedings of the 1971 IFIP Congress. In the March 1975 *Communications*, Floyd and Rivest present a selection algorithm that uses just $N+K+O(\sqrt{N})$ comparisons. Their algorithm is close to the theoretical optimum, and their code runs like the wind.

APPENDIX 1: **THE C AND AWK LANGUAGES**

Many of the programs in this book are written in an Algol-like pseudocode. Several places, though, called for real programs. I chose to illustrate the profilers discussed in Section 1 in the C language. The Awk language is used heavily in Columns 2 and 3, and is used slightly in Columns 1, 9 and 13.

1.1 The C Language

There are many texts and reference manuals for C. The first, and still my personal favorite, is *The C Programming Language* by Kernighan and Ritchie, published by Prentice-Hall in 1978; a second edition appeared in 1988. This section sketches a few of the C-isms that appear in Column 1.

The statement a=b assigns the value of b to a, and the expression a==b is true if the two variables are equal. The expression a%b is the remainder when a is divided by b, so 10%7 is 3. The `printf` routine provides a formatted print statement.

The statement i++ increments the integer i. The ++ operator can also be used in expressions. If j is 6 then the expression x[j++] yields x[6] and sets j to 7, while x[++j] sets j to 7 and yields x[7]. The decrement operator -- is similar: x[--j] sets j to 5 and yields x[5].

The `if` statement has the form

```
if (expression) statement
```

The Pascal loop

```
for i := a to b do statement
```

is written in C as

```
for (i = a; i <= b; i++) statement
```

171

1.2 The Awk Language

The definitive reference for Awk is *The AWK Programming Language* by
Aho, Kernighan and Weinberger, cited in Section 2.6. Much of Awk's syntax is
borrowed from C. In particular, all of the constructs described in the previous
section also appear in Awk.

Simple Awk programs can perform interesting computations. Here's a complete program to compute the base-two logarithms of a file of input numbers.

```
{ print log($1)/log(2) }
```

Given the input file

```
2
16
4
10
```

it produces the output file

```
1
4
2
3.32193
```

The program illustrates several important Awk services. The `print` statement
enclosed in braces is implicitly iterated over all lines in the input file; the programmer needn't worry about the details of the input loop. Additionally, Awk
breaks the input lines into fields. The first field is called $1, the second $2, etc.
The expression in the `print` statement uses arithmetic and the built-in `log`
function.

Many of the Awk programs that we will study in this book have the following structure.

```
BEGIN { preprocessing }
      { action for each input line }
END   { postprocessing }
```

The preprocessing is done before the first line of the file is read, and the postprocessing is done after the last line has been read. Any of the three parts may
be omitted. Awk uses braces for grouping statements; Pascal uses `begin` and
`end` for the task.

In general, an Awk program consists of "pattern-action" pairs. If the input
line matches the pattern on the left, then the code on the right is executed; that
process is repeated for each pattern on each input line. BEGIN and END are
special patterns that match before and after the file has been read.

Input lines for the next program contain two fields. The first is a positive number and the second is a string. The output is the maximum number in the file and its associated string.

```
$1 > maxval { maxval = $1; maxname = $2 }
END         { print "Maximum value: " maxval
              print "Associated name: " maxname
            }
```

Awk initializes variables at their first use (numbers to zero, strings to empty), so the above program needn't initialize maxval explicitly. The two statements in the first action are separated by a semicolon; statements on separate lines don't require the semicolon.

The next program computes the mean of the numbers in the input file, which may contain several numbers on a line. When Awk processes the input line, it stores the number of fields in the variable NF.

```
{ for (i = 1; i <= NF; i++) {
    n++
    sum = sum + $i
  }
}
END { print "Average of", n, "numbers is", sum/n }
```

Awk conveniently converts variables between numbers and strings at run time. In most programs in this book it should be clear which is which; details on the policy are in the Awk book.

An Awk function is much like a C function, except that it lacks variable declarations. The way to declare a local variable in a function, therefore, is to place it in the parameter list. I put the genuine parameters first in the parameter list; local variables come next, separated by two spaces. A function may return a value with the return statement.

APPENDIX 2: **A SUBROUTINE LIBRARY**

This appendix contains the subroutine library described in Section 3.3. The set algorithms operate on the array $x[1..n]$. When the program was executed, all tests were passed.

The selection algorithm `select` is described in Column 15. The other subroutines are derived and formally proved correct in the following sections of my 1986 book *Programming Pearls*:

FUNCTION NAME	ALGORITHM	SECTION
qsort	Quick sort	10.2
isort	Insertion sort	10.1
siftup	Heaps	12.2
siftdown	Heaps	12.2
hsort	Heap sort	12.4
pqinit	Priority queue initialization	12.3
pqinsert	Priority queue insertion	12.3
pqextractmin	Priority queue extraction	12.3
ssearch	Sequential search	2.2
bsearch	Binary search	2.2

The complete Awk program appears on the following pages. The set algorithms come first, followed by the testing routines, followed by the main routine.

```
# UTILITY ROUTINES AND SET ALGORITHMS



function swap(i, j,  t) { # x[i] :=: x[j]
    t = x[i]; x[i] = x[j]; x[j] = t
}



function randint(l, u) { # rand int in l..u
    return l + int((u-l+1)*rand())
} ti



function select(k,  l, u, i, t, m) {
        # post: x[1..k-1] <= x[k] <= x[k+1..n]
        # bugs: n**2 time if x[1]=...=x[n]
    l = 1; u = n
    while (l < u) {
        # x[1..l-1] <= x[l..u] <= x[u+1..n]
        swap(l, randint(l,u))
        t = x[l]
        m = l
        for (i = l+1; i <= u; i++) {
            # x[l+1..m] < t and x[m+1..i-1] >= t
            if (x[i] < t) swap(++m,i)
        }
        swap(l,m)
        # x[1..m-1] <= x[m] <= x[m+1..u]
        if (m <= k) l = m+1
        if (m >= k) u = m-1
    }
}



function qsort(l, u,  i, t, m) {
        # post: sorted(l,u)
        # bugs: n**2 time if x[1]=...=x[n]
    if (l < u) {
        swap(l, randint(l, u))
        t = x[l]
        m = l
        for (i = l+1; i <= u; i++) {
            # x[l+1..m] < t and x[m+1..i-1] >= t
            if (x[i] < t) swap(++m, i)
        }
        swap(l, m)
        # x[1..m-1] <= x[m] <= x[m+1..u]
        qsort(l, m-1)
        qsort(m+1, u)
    }
}
```

```
function isort(  i, j) {
        # post: sorted(1,n)
    for (i = 2; i <= n; i++) {
        # sorted(1, i-1)
        j = i
        while (j > 1 && x[j-1] > x[j]) {
            swap(j-1, j)
            j--
        }
    }
}


function siftup(l, u,  i, p) {
        # pre  maxheap(l,u-1)
        # post maxheap(l,u)
    i = u
    while (1) {
        # maxheap(l,u) except between
        #  i and its parent
        if (i <= 1) break
        p = int(i/2)
        if (x[p] >= x[i]) break
        swap(p, i)
        i = p
    }
}


function siftdown(l, u,  i, c) {
        # pre  maxheap(l+1,u)
        # post maxheap(l,u)
    i = l
    while (1) {
        # maxheap(l,u) except between
        #  i and its children
        c = 2*i
        if (c > u) break
        if (c+1 <= u && x[c+1] > x[c]) c++
        if (x[i] >= x[c]) break
        swap(c, i)
        i = c
    }
}


function hsort(  i) {
        # post sorted(1,n)
    for (i = int(n/2); i >= 1; i--)
        siftdown(i, n)
    for (i = n; i >= 2; i--) {
        swap(1, i); siftdown(1, i-1)
    }
}


function pqinit(i) {
    pqmax = i
    n = 0
}
```

```
function pqinsert(t) {
        # post t is added to set
    assert(n < pqmax)
    x[++n] = t
    siftup(1, n)
}


function pqextractmax(  t) {
        # pre   set isn't empty
        # post max is deleted and returned
    assert(n >= 1)
    t = x[1]; x[1] = x[n--]
    siftdown(1, n)
    return t
}


function ssearch(t,  i) {
        # post result=0      => x[1..n]  != t
        #       1<=result<=n => x[result] = t
    i = 1
    while (i <= n && x[i] != t) i++
    if (i <= n) return i; else return 0
}


function bsearch(t,  l,u,m) {
        # pre  x[1] <= x[2] <= ... <= x[n]
        # post result=0      => x[1..n]  != t
        #       1<=result<=n => x[result] = t
    l = 1; u = n
    while (l <= u) {
        # t is in x[1..n] => t is in x[l..u]
        m = int((l+u)/2)
        if      (x[m] < t) l = m+1
        else if (x[m] > t) u = m-1
        else return m
    }
    return 0
}

# TESTING ROUTINES


function genequal(  i) { # fill x
    for (i = 1; i <= n; i++) x[i] = 1
}


function geninorder(  i) { # fill x
    for (i = 1; i <= n; i++) x[i] = i
}


function scramble(  i) { # shuffle x
    for (i = 1; i < n; i++)
        swap(i, randint(i, n))
}
```

```
function assert(cond) {
    if (!cond) {
        errcnt++
        print "   >> assert failed <<"
    }
}


function checkselect(k,  i) {
    for (i = 1;   i <  k; i++)
        assert(x[i] <= x[k])
    for (i = k+1; i <= n; i++)
        assert(x[i] >= x[k])
}


function checksort(  i) {
    for (i = 1; i < n;  i++)
        assert(x[i] <= x[i+1])
}


function clearsubs(  i) { # clear array x
    for (i in x) delete x[i]
}


function checksubs(  i,c) { # alters x
        # error if subscripts not in 1..n
    for (i = 1; i <= n; i++) delete x[i]
    for (i in x) c++
    assert(c == 0)
}


function sort() { # call proper sort
    if       (sortname == "qsort") qsort(1, n)
    else if (sortname == "hsort") hsort()
    else if (sortname == "isort") isort()
    else print "invalid sort name"
}


function testsort(name,  i, nfac) {
    sortname = name
    print "  pathological tests"
    for (n = 0; n <= bign; n++) {
        print "   n=", n
        clearsubs()
        geninorder(); sort(); checksort()
        for (i = 1; i <= n/2; i++) swap(i, n+1-i)
        sort(); checksort()
        genequal(); sort(); checksort()
        checksubs()
    }
```

```
        print "  random tests"
        nfac = 1
        for (n = 1; n <= smalln; n++) {
            print "    n=", n
            nfac = nfac*n
            clearsubs()
            geninorder();
            for (i = 1; i <= nfac; i++) {
                scramble(); sort(); checksort()
            }
            checksubs()
        }
    }


    function search(t) { # call proper search
        if      (searchname == "bsearch")
            return bsearch(t)
        else if (searchname == "ssearch")
            return ssearch(t)
        else print "invalid search name"
    }


    function testsearch(name,  i) {
        searchname = name
        for (n = 0; n <= bign; n++) {
            print "    n=", n
            clearsubs()
            geninorder()
            for (i = 1; i <= n; i++) {
                assert(search(i)    == i)
                assert(search(i-.5) == 0)
                assert(search(i+.5) == 0)
            }
            genequal()
            assert(search(0.5) == 0)
            if (n > 0) assert(search(1) >= 1)
            assert(search(1) <= n)
            assert(search(1.5) == 0)
            checksubs()
        }
    }


    BEGIN { # MAIN PROGRAM
    bign = 12
    smalln = 5
    print "testing assert -- should fail"
        assert(1 == 0)
```

```
print "testing select"
    for (n = 0; n <= bign; n++) {
        print "   n=", n
        clearsubs()
        for (i = 1; i <= n; i++) {
            geninorder()
            select(i)
            checkselect(i)
        }
        for (i = 1; i <= n; i++) {
            scramble()
            select(i)
            checkselect(i)
        }
        genequal()
        for (i = 1; i <= n; i++) {
            select(i)
            checkselect(i)
        }
        checksubs()
    }



print "testing quick sort"
    testsort("qsort")
print "testing insertion sort"
    testsort("isort")
print "testing heap sort"
    testsort("hsort")



print "testing priority queues"
    for (m = 0; m <= bign; m++) {
        # m is max heap size
        print "   m=", m
        clearsubs()
        pqinit(m)
        for (i = 1; i <= m; i++)
            pqinsert(i)
        for (i = m; i >= 1, i--)
            assert(pqextractmax() == i)
        assert(n == 0)
        pqinit(m)
        for (i = m; i >= 1; i--)
            pqinsert(i)
        for (i = m; i >= 1; i--)
            assert(pqextractmax() == i)
        assert(n == 0)
        pqinit(m)
        for (i = 1; i <= m; i++)
            pqinsert(1)
        for (i = m; i >= 1; i--)
            assert(pqextractmax() == 1)
        assert(n == 0)
        n = m; checksubs()
    }
```

```
print "testing sequential search"
    testsearch("ssearch")
print "testing binary search"
    testsearch("bsearch")
print "total errors (1 expected):", errcnt
if (errcnt > 1) print ">>>> TEST FAILED <<<<"
}
```

SOLUTIONS TO SELECTED PROBLEMS

Solutions for Column 1

1. The problem can be rephrased as asking how many assignments this routine makes after the array $X[1..N]$ has been sprinkled with random real numbers chosen uniformly over $[0,1]$.

```
Max := X[1]
for I := 2 to N do
    if X[I] > Max then
        Max := X[I]
```

A simple argument assumes that `if` statements are executed about half the time, so the program will make roughly $N/2$ assignments. I profiled the program for ten runs with $N=1000$, and the number of assignments were, in sorted order:

    4   4   5   5   6   7   8   8   8   9

In Section 1.2.10 of *Fundamental Algorithms*, Knuth shows that the algorithm makes H_N-1 assignments, on the average, where

$$H_N = 1 + 1/2 + 1/3 + \cdots + 1/N$$

is the Nth harmonic number. For $N=1000$, this analysis gives an expectation of 6.485; the average of the ten experiments is 6.4.

2. The following C program implements a Sieve of Eratosthenes for computing all primes less than n. Its primary data structure is the array x of n bits, which are initialized to 1. As each prime is discovered, all of its multiples in the array are set to 0. The next prime is the next 1 bit in the array. The profile shows that there are 9592 primes less than 100,000, and that the algorithm made about $2.57N$ assignments. In general, the algorithm makes about $N \log \log N$ assignments; the analysis involves the density of prime

183

numbers and the harmonic numbers mentioned in Solution 1.1. Here is the profiled code:

```
              main()
              {    int i, p, n;
                   char x[100002];
      1            n = 100000;
      1            for (i = 1; i <= n; i++)
 100000                x[i] = 1;
      1            x[1] = 0; x[n+1] = 1;
      1            p = 2;
   9593            while (p <= n) {
   9592                printf("%d\n", p);
   9592                for (i = 2*p; i <= n; i = i+p)
 256808                    x[i] = 0;
   9592                do
  99999                    p++;
  99999                while (x[p] == 0);
                   }
              }
```

For faster implementations of prime sieves, see the *Communications of the ACM* papers by Mairson (September 1977), Gries and Misra (December 1978), and Pritchard (January 1981), or Pritchard's "Linear prime-number sieves: A family tree" in *Science of Computer Programming*, vol. 9, pp. 17–35, 1987.

3. A simple statement-count profiler increments a counter at each statement. One can decrease both the memory requirements and the run time of a profiled program by making do with fewer counters. For instance, one might associate a counter with each basic block in the program's flow graph. One can further reduce the number of counters by using "Kirchhoff's first law": if you have a counter for an if-then-else statement and one for the then branch, then you don't need one for the else branch.

6. The for loop in function prime could potentially give an infinite loop. To show that the loop always terminates, one must prove that if P is a prime, then there is another prime less than P^2. That theorem is true, but the proof of the theorem is hard.

Solutions for Column 2

3. In Exercise 2.2.3−23 of his *Fundamental Algorithms*, Knuth shows how to print a cycle in the input graph, if one exists.

4. Here is a cyclic graph induced by a three-dimensional scene.

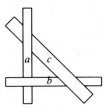

It is cyclic because a must be drawn before b, b before c, and c before a. If each object in the scene is flat (that is, it has a single z value), and all z values are distinct, then the z values provide a total ordering and the scene has no cycles.

5a. This Awk program inserts 1000 random numbers into an initially empty binary search tree, then traverses it.

```
BEGIN { <<<1>>>   n = 1000; root = null = -1
        for (i = 1; i <= n; i++)
            root = insert(root, int(n*rand()))
        traverse(root); exit
}
function insert(p, x) { <<<11840>>>
        if (p == null) { <<<632>>>
            val[p = ++nodecount] = x
            lson[p] = rson[p] = null
        } else if (x < val[p]) { <<<4847>>>
            lson[p] = insert(lson[p], x)
        } else if (x > val[p]) { <<<5993>>>
            rson[p] = insert(rson[p], x)
        } else { <<<368>>>   }
        return p
}
function traverse(p) { <<<1265>>>
        if (p != null) { <<<633>>>
            traverse(lson[p])
            print val[p]
            traverse(rson[p])
        }
}
```

The numbers were produced by the Awk profiler described in Section 1.4. The BEGIN block called the `insert` function 1000 times; it inserted 632 new numbers in the tree and returned 368 times because the number was there already. Each insertion took about 11.8 recursive calls, on the average.

5b. This Awk program uses depth-first search to solve reachability. The typical input line contains a predecessor, successor pair; the sequence of pairs defines a directed graph. (The topological sort program used the same format.)

When the input line is *reach x*, the program prints all nodes that can be reached from *x*, using a recursive depth-first search.

```
function visit(node,  i) {
    if (visited[node] == 0) {
        visited[node] = 1
        print "   " node
        for (i = 1; i <= succct[node]; i++)
            visit(succlist[node, i])
    }
}
$1 == "reach" { print "Nodes reached from " $2
                for (i in succct)
                    visited[i] = 0
                visit($2)
              }
$1 != "reach" { succlist[$1, ++succct[$1]] = $2
                succct[$2] = 0 + succct[$2] # make it exist
              }
```

The AWK Programming Language by Aho, Weinberger and Kernighan (cited in Section 2.6) presents algorithms for random sentence generation in Section 5.1 and a depth-first-search implementation of topological sort in Section 7.3.

6. Associative arrays can be implemented with data structures for "symbol tables". Relevant structures include binary search trees and sorted and unsorted sequences. The method of choice in most systems, though, is the structure Awk uses: hash tables. Solutions 13.2 and 13.6 survey several implementations of symbol tables.

Solutions for Column 3

Solutions 1, 2 and 3 refer to this Awk testbed for experimenting on heaps. More details on the code can be found in Column 12 of my 1986 book *Programming Pearls*.

```
function maxheap(l, u,  i) { # 1 if a heap
    for (i = 2*l; i <= u; i++)
        if (x[int(i/2)] < x[i])
            return 0
    return 1
}

function assert(cond, errmsg) {
    if (!cond) {
        print ">>> Assertion failed <<<"
        print "    Error message: ", errmsg
    }
}
```

```
function siftdown(l, u,  i, c, t) {
        # precondition   maxheap(l+1,u)
        # postcondition  maxheap(l,u)
assert(maxheap(l+1, u), "siftdown precondition")
    i = l
    while (1) {
        # maxheap(l,u) except between i and its children
        c = 2*i
        if (c > u) break
        if (c+1 <= u && x[c+1] > x[c]) c++
        if (x[i] >= x[c]) break
        t = x[i];  x[i] = x[c];  x[c] = t  # swap i, c
        i = c
    }
assert(maxheap(l, u), "siftdown postcondition")
}

function draw(i, s) {
    if (i <= n) {
        print i ":", s, x[i]
        draw(2*i,   s "    ")
        draw(2*i+1, s "    ")
    }
}
$1 == "draw"   { draw(1, "") }
$1 == "down"   { siftdown($2, $3) }
$1 == "assert" { assert(maxheap($2, $3), "cmd") }
$1 == "x"      { x[$2] = $3 }
$1 == "n"      { n = $2 }
```

1. The recursive **draw** routine uses indentation to print the implicit tree structure of the heap (the second parameter in the recursive is the indentation string **s**; each call appends four spaces to it).

2. The modified **assert** routine includes a string variable that provides information about the assertion that failed. Some systems provide an assertion facility that automatically gives the source file and the line number of the invalid assertion.

3. The **siftdown** routine uses the **assert** and **maxheap** routines to test the pre- and post-conditions on entry and exit. The **maxheap** routine requires $O(U-L)$ time, so the **assert** calls should be removed from the production version of the code.

4. The tests in Appendix 2 missed a bug in my first **siftup** procedure. I mistakenly initialized **i** with the incorrect assignment **i=n** rather than with the correct assignment **i=u**. In all my tests, though, **u** and **n** were equal, so they did not identify the bug.

6. Section 15.3 describes experiments on the running time of Hoare's algorithm for selecting the kth-smallest element in a set.

8. To test that a sort routine permutes its input, we could copy the input into a separate array, sort that by a trusted method, and compare the two arrays after the new routine has finished. An alternative method uses only a few bytes of storage, but sometimes makes a mistake: it uses the sum of the elements in the array as a *signature* of those elements. Changing a subset of the elements will change the sum with high probability. (Summing involves problems related to word size and non-associativity of floating-point addition; other signatures, such as exclusive or, avoid these problems.)

Solutions for Column 4

2. In Section 3.9 of *The UNIX Programming Environment* (Prentice-Hall, 1984), Kernighan and Pike present a program named `bundle`. The command

        bundle file1 file2 file3

   produces a UNIX shell file. When executed, it writes copies of all the files in the bundle.

3. A self-reproducing program exists in any universal model of computation. The proof uses the Recursion Theorem and the *s-m-n* Theorem of recursive function theory. Hackers have long delighted in writing self-reproducing programs in real languages; Fortran and C seem to be particularly popular. The problem is easier if you allow the program to self-reproduce on the error output. If you start with a small file (say, the single word junk), and then iteratively feed the error messages printed by the compiler as input back to the compiler, the process usually converges quickly.

4. The UNIX file system does not classify files by type, but several programs use the contents of files as an implicit self-description. The `file` command, for instance, examines a file and guesses whether the contents represent ASCII text, program text, shell commands, etc. In their book cited in Solution 2, Kernighan and Pike present a program called `doctype` that reads a Troff input file and deduces what language preprocessors (such as Pic, Tbl, etc.) need to be run on it.

5. Examples of name-value pairs include PL/1's `GET DATA` statement and Fortran's `NAMELIST`. Arrays and functions both map names to values.

7. A general principle states that the output of a program should be suitable for input to the program. This is especially important for programs that are pipes and in window systems that allow output to be selected and re-entered as input with a few mouse motions.

Solutions for Column 5

1. Since the file was so small, I suggested re-keying the data from a readily available listing. Even I can enter digits at the rate of one per second, which translates to three records per minute or two hundred per hour. Having a data entry clerk re-key the data using familiar tools should therefore take less than two hours and cost less than fifty dollars. An automated solution would require substantial software on both PCs (I would search hard for packages before writing code myself), as well as the purchase of modems. Although the high-tech solution is clearly preferable for large volumes of data, the simple solution was superior for the problem at hand.

2. Lynn Jelinski received the following note from her father, Geoffrey Woodard,

   > According to legend, an apprentice plumber new on the job is sent to look for a left-handed pipe wrench.

   > Edison assigned his new employees the job of determining the volume of a light bulb, which is extremely difficult to calculate from measurements, but simple to determine by displacement in a graduated cylinder.

   > Somewhere, I heard that at Bell Labs, the first assignment was to improve the telephone's coiled receiver cord. The punch line is that a one-cent change (a redesign does away with the cord by keeping the mouthpiece and receiver nearer the line terminus) translates into savings of millions of dollars. Anyway, be warned.

   What similar hazing rituals does (or should) your company have?

3. I was premature in leaping to a computerized solution. As soon as I regained my wits, I suggested that the psychologist write the six permutations of {1,2,3} on the six faces of a wooden block, and likewise put the stress levels on another block. When a subject walked in the room, the experimenter could generate the random permutations by rolling the two dice.

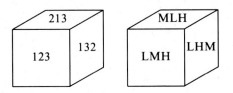

   Although I was delighted by this simple, elegant and effective solution, the psychologist really wanted the authority of "The Computer" behind the experiments. I wrote the program, on the condition that I could tell the story in this book.

4. Because `sqrt` is a monotone increasing function, we can remove the square

root from the code in the loop, and take a single square root after the loop. Many programmers have a conceptual block against removing the square root routine.

Solutions for Column 7

3. On many microcomputer Basic interpreters, the cost of accessing a variable is proportional to its position in the symbol table. Variables used near the front of the program are therefore cheaper to access than those first used late in execution. On machines with instruction caches, a minor change can slide an inner loop out of the cache and increase total time by twenty percent. The week before I first wrote this column, a colleague squeezed a factor of ten from an Awk program I had written by changing the quotation marks surrounding a pattern to be slashes (I didn't appreciate a subtle semantic distinction).

4. One could estimate the local death rate by counting death notices in a newspaper and estimating the population of the area they represent. An easier approach uses Little's Law and an estimate of life expectancy; if the life expectancy is 70 years, for instance, then 1/70 or 1.4% of the population dies each year.

5. Peter Denning's proof of Little's Law has two parts. "First, define $\lambda = A/T$, the arrival rate, where A is the number of arrivals during an observation period of length T. Define $X = C/T$, the output rate, where C is the number of completions during T. Let $n(t)$ denote the number in the system at time t in $[0, T]$. Let W be the area under $n(t)$, in units of 'item-seconds', representing the total aggregated waiting time over all items in the system during the observation period. The mean response time per item completed is defined as $R = W/C$, in units of (item-seconds)/(item). The mean number in the system is the average height of $n(t)$ and is $L = W/T$, in units of (item-seconds)/(second). It is now obvious that $L = RX$. This formulation is in terms of the output rate only. There is no requirement for 'flow balance', i.e., that flow in equal flow out (in symbols, $\lambda = X$). If you add that assumption, the formula becomes $L = \lambda \times R$, which is the form encountered in queueing and system theory."

6. Peter Denning writes: "Suppose you have a network of servers. Let V_i denote the mean number of times each job uses (visits) server i. Then $V_1 + \cdots + V_N$ denotes the total number of job-steps in an average job. The overall system throughput, X_0, is related to the local throughput at server i by the 'forced flow' law: $X_i = V_i \times X_0$. Let R_0 denote the response time experienced by a job and L_0 denote the average number of jobs in the system. Little's formula says that the system's response time is $R_0 = L_0/X_0$. But $L_0 = L_1 + \cdots + L_N$, where L_i is the mean number of jobs at server i;

$L_i=R_i\times X_i$, where R_i is the mean response time per visit to server i. Using $X_i/X_0=V_i$ from the fixed flow law, you get $R_0 = R_1\times V_1+\cdots+R_N\times V_N$. This is intuitively true, but easily and rigorously proved using Little's Law twice."

7. Bruce Weide writes: "In the original case, the 'system' is the queue plus the server. Using the notation of Solution 5, R is the average time a customer spends in the queue and in service, and L is the average number of customers in the queue and in service. So by Little's Law, we know $L=RX$, where X is the output rate of the server. But X is also the output rate of the queue, since a customer goes directly from the queue to the server whenever another leaves the server. Considering the queue by itself to be the 'system' and defining L_Q as the average number in the queue and R_Q as the average time spent in the queue alone, we see that $L_Q=R_QX$. The desired relationship, then, is that the ratios L/R and L_Q/R_Q are equal."

8. Bruce Weide offers this solution. "One way to solve this problem considers two queueing systems. The first is the queue of jobs awaiting execution, and the second is the computer system itself. By Little's Law, the second system has the output rate of jobs, $X = L/R$. Here, $L=10$ jobs (because there is always a backlog of work, the system will always have the maximum 10 jobs in it, so 10 is also the average number of jobs in the system). The average time is $R=20$ seconds, so X must be $1/2$ job per second. This is also the arrival rate of jobs to the second system — flow balance is satisfied because L is constant, which means every job completing execution is immediately replaced by the next job. Now the output rate of the first system must also be $1/2$ job/second. We should therefore expect the 99 jobs ahead of ours to be out of the way after 198 seconds. Then our job completes 20 seconds later, for a total wait of 218 seconds."

Solutions for Column 9

1. Section 6.3 of *The AWK Programming Language* describes a little language for generating UNIX sort commands.

2. The UNIX system uses regular expressions in the ed editor and grep pattern matcher.

3. Section 4.1 describes a little language for describing bibliographic references.

4. Section 6.1 of *The AWK Programming Language* describes an assembler and interpreter implemented in a few dozen lines of Awk. Stacks are used in languages ranging from the machine code for hand-held calculators (such as HP machines) to little languages for typesetting (Postscript) to general-purpose languages (Forth) to hardware (Burroughs machines).

6. When Mark Kernighan was 11 years old, he started to write a music program in Basic with this structure:

```
1 ' Play a tune
100 POKE 36874, 262
110 FOR I=1 to 1000: NEXT I
120 POKE 36875, 183
130 FOR I=1 TO 2000: NEXT I
140 POKE 36875, 190
150 FOR I=1 TO 1000: NEXT I
160 POKE 36874, 240
170 FOR I=1 TO 1000: NEXT I
    ...
```

Line 100 generates a tone by "poking" a value into location 36874, line 110 waits while the tone plays, and line 120 plays a tone through a second generator by poking a value into location 36875. A nudge from his father, Brian Kernighan, encouraged Mark to consider the error of his ways. He then rewrote the program to use the microscopic music language defined in the remarks.

```
1 ' 1..99      => Delay
2 ' 100..999   => Tone 1
3 ' 1000..1999 => Tone 2
10 DATA 262, 1, 1183, 2, 1190, 1, 240, 1, ...
100 READ X
110 IF X >= 100 THEN GOTO 140
120     FOR I=1 TO X*1000: NEXT I
130     GOTO 100
140 IF X >= 1000 THEN GOTO 170
150     POKE 36874, X
160     GOTO 100
170 ' 1000 <= X <= 1999
180     POKE 36875, X-1000
190     GOTO 100
```

8. Morally acceptable strategies for coping with linguistic mistakes range from single error detection to multiple error detection to error correction. (Ignoring errors is, of course, grossly immoral and will therefore not be considered.) Single error detection reports the first error in the input and then halts; this strategy is easy to implement and useful for debugging. Multiple error detection is more useful because it flags many errors; it is harder to implement because the parser must untangle itself from one error before looking for the next. Error correction does what someone thinks the user really wanted to do; it is very difficult to implement and can be irksome when it guesses incorrectly.

Solutions for Column 10

2. Three variations of selection sort are shown in this figure, in which the array is represented horizontally and time proceeds down the vertical axis.

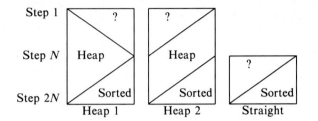

The left diagram shows a simple Heapsort, which builds the heap by sifting each element up the partially built heap. The middle Heapsort has the same second phase, but builds the heap right-to-left by sifting elements down (Appendix 2 uses this version). The right diagram shows a straight insertion sort; it does not build a heap, which avoids the construction cost but greatly increases the cost of each selection.

3. The problem asked how programs should be typeset to achieve the three goals of correctness, consistency, and clarity.

Correctness. The best way to get a correct program in a document is to start with a correct program on a computer. Life is easiest when one can test and typeset the program from the same source file. I do that whenever possible. In some columns, however, I present the algorithms in a pseudocode based on Pascal but I implement and test them in C. I therefore write the C programs in a form as close as possible to the final pseudocode, and then use a text editor to make the remaining changes (I know — I should write a program to do the job).

Consistency. Programmers should be consistent about little details such as capitalization and indentation. Even better than adhering to your own standard, follow one that already exists in the field. When I present C programs, for instance, I try to use the format employed by Kernighan and Ritchie in *The C Programming Language.*

Clarity. Many systems, such as Don Knuth's WEB system, produce clear programs by varying fonts: **bold** for keywords, *italic* for variables, `typewriter` for text strings, roman for comments, etc. The programs in this book are typeset in `typewriter` font: that fixed-size font reflects what most programmers (myself included) see on their terminals, and is still readable even when shrunk to a fairly small size (see, for instance, Appendix 2).

Solutions for Column 11

1. The last graph in Section 11.1 places two graphs side-by-side to save space. Because the graphs have a common *x* scale and distinct *y* scales, it would be more useful to place one graph above the other.

3. The left graph plots weight in pounds as a function of miles per gallon. It shows a correlation, but fails to suggest a general law.

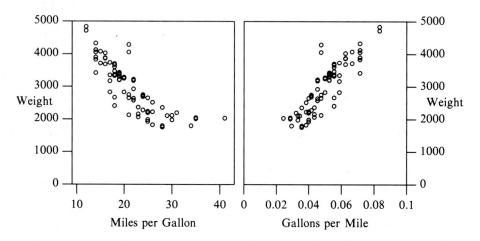

Paul Tukey of Bell Communications Research suggested that we should instead plot weight as a function of gallons per mile, the reciprocal of mileage. His plot is presented in the right graph. It shows that the two variables are related almost linearly, which explains a hyperbolic trend in the left graph. Furthermore, the regression line passes through the origin. The two outliers near 4000 pounds and 21 mpg (roughly .048 gallons per mile) are the Oldsmobile 98 and the Cadillac Seville. They are heavier than other cars with similar mileage ratings, or alternatively, they have excellent mileage compared to other cars of their weight.

4. Solution 3 shows that re-expressing coordinate axes so that data points lie near a straight line can make a relationship more obvious. We will consider the relationship $y=a\times x^b$. Taking the logarithm of both sides of the equation gives

$$\log y = \log a + b \log x$$

If we plot the curve on the new axes $x' = \log x$ and $y' = \log y$ then we see the linear relationship

$$y' = \log a + bx'$$

Plotting the relationship $y=a\times b^x$ with y transformed to $y' = \log y$ gives

$$y' = \log a + (\log b)x$$

For the relationship $y = a\sqrt{x}+b$ we re-express $x'=\sqrt{x}$ so $y=ax'+b$. For more details on transforming axes to highlight relationships, see J. W. Tukey's *Exploratory Data Analysis*, published in 1977 by Addison-Wesley; Chapters 5 and 6 are especially relevant.

5. This Basic program displays the random number generator $RND\,(1)$, which returns a pseudo-random real chosen uniformly between zero and one. It divides the unit interval into the number of bins specified by the user, and then grows a histogram of the number of randoms in each bin (the array element $B\,(I)$ counts the randoms in the Ith bin).

```
10 INPUT "Bins"; N
20 DIM B(N-1) ' N bins, 0..N-1
30 FOR I=0 TO N-1: B(I)=0: NEXT I
40 CLS ' Clear screen
50 I=CINT(N*RND(1))
60   B(I)=B(I)+1
70   SET(B(I),I)
80   GOTO 50
```

The SET subroutine turns on the pixel specified by its two parameters, and CINT truncates a real number (so CINT(7.9) is 7). The infinite loop in lines 50 through 80 is terminated by hitting "BREAK" or by accessing a pixel off the screen (although infinite loops are usually poor practice, I find them handy for quick programs like this). The Basic system I tested exhibited appropriate behavior: the bin sizes were close to one another, but not too close.

Solutions for Column 12

1b. It is easy for the user to supply the response numbers, and their presence makes it more convenient to look up particular responses in a hard-copy listing of a survey description.

3b. Even though the new graph contains the same information as the first graph in Section 12.3, I find the old version superior in several ways. The new version has some minor problems that could be fixed easily. Aligning the numbers at the left of their respective boxes would reduce visual clutter and make them easier to compare. Rounding to integer percentages would also reduce clutter, without sacrificing significant information.

Small fixes can't solve the main problem with the new graph: its basic form is clumsy. It has half again as many boxes as its predecessor, and their placement makes them more difficult to compare. Quantitatively, the previous graph uses a single line to denote 50%; this graph would require three lines for the same job. The first graph grouped the data in the same vertical order as the other graphs (Total, Male, Female) so the reader can transfer that pattern among the various graphs, while this graph requires a new pattern. Although the person who prepared the new graph was excited by its razzle-dazzle, the users found it cluttered and distracting. The company went back to the old form.

3c. John Tukey of Bell Labs and Princeton University kindly commented on the second bar graph in Section 12.3. He had several suggestions regarding the execution of the graph. Since the "Don't Know" bars point towards the "Poor" and "Very Poor" bars, the space between them seems to be significant (the first graph in Section 12.3 uses such a space to represent a quantity). Because the space has no significance in this graph, Tukey suggested that the "Don't Know" bars point right to remove the implication. The "Excellent" and "Very Poor" categories represent strong feelings that are not emphasized in the above graph; Tukey proposed shading those bars to increase their visual impact. Finally, he suggested that reducing the size of the numbers would reduce graphical clutter without decreasing the readability of the graph.

Tukey also suggested a fundamental change in the form of the graph to underscore the two parts of its message: the relative rating of the various officials and the "gender gap" between the perception of men and women. He suggested regrouping the bars in the graph to tell those two stories in order. Combining his ideas yields the following graph, which I think is far superior to mine.

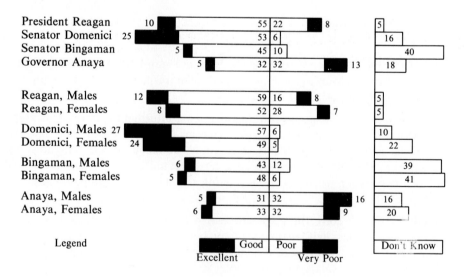

Solutions for Column 13

2. Bob Floyd described several possible data structures to implement the set S in Algorithm F2: "A bit array is appropriate if N is no more than perhaps 100 M; if b is the number of bits per word, then the run time is virtually constant at $O(M) + O(N/b)$.

   "For larger N, use an array of size near M indexed by the high order bits of the data, of pointers to sorted linked lists containing (the low order bits of) the data. Mean execution time is $O(M)$, variance is $O(M)$, and maximum is $O(M^2)$.

   "A cautious implementation uses a balanced ordered tree. Mean and worst-case times are $O(M \log M)$, with small variance."

3. A data structure that is efficient for Algorithm S might be slow when used in Algorithm F2. When $M=N$, for instance, a binary search tree gives logarithmic expected search time in Algorithm S. In Algorithm F2, though, the elements are inserted in increasing order, so the binary search tree degrades into a linked list with linear search time.

5. Any algorithm for generating a random M-element permutation from $1..N$ must use at least

$$\log_2 (N \times N{-}1 \times \cdots \times N{-}M{+}1) = \sum_{I=N-M+1}^{N} \log_2 I$$

   random bits. Algorithm P consumes

$$\sum_{I=N-M+1}^{N} \left\lceil \log_2 I \right\rceil$$

   random bits, so it is within M bits of optimal.

   Doug McIlroy developed this algorithm to store the G-th combination of M of N items in array A:

```
procedure Comb(N, M, G, A)
    D := 1
    while M > 0 do
        T := C(N - D, M - 1)
        if G - T < 0 then
            M := M - 1
            A[M] := D
        else
            G := G - T
        D := D + 1
```

   The function C(N,M) returns $\binom{N}{M}$. Both the array A and the integer G use a "zero-origin": the array is indexed over $0..M-1$ and the first permutation corresponds to $G=0$. One can therefore generate a random M-element sub-set of $1..N$ with the call

```
Comb(N, M, RandInt(0, C(N,M)-1), A)
```

This method uses precisely the optimal number of random bits.

6. Floyd writes, "An appropriate data structure for the sequence S in Algo-rithm P is a hash table with a linked list connecting the entries. If the hash table size is about $2M$, the expected running time is $O(M)$. A cautious ver-sion of this representation is a balanced ordered tree with a linked list run-ning through it, for expected and worst case times $O(M \log M)$."

8. Burstall and Darlington describe a system for transforming recursive pro-grams in *Acta Informatica 6*, 1, pp. 41–60 (1976) and in *JACM 24*, 1, pp. 44–67 (January 1977).

9. Column 11 of my 1986 book *Programming Pearls* surveys several algorithms for generating random samples. It describes, for instance, this program from Section 3.4.2 of Knuth's *Seminumerical Algorithms*:

```
Select := M; Remaining := N
for I := 1 to N do
    if RandReal(0,1) < Select/Remaining then
        print I; Select := Select-1
    Remaining := Remaining-1
```

That column also describes several implementations for the set S that is the primary data structure in Algorithm S.

Solutions for Column 14

1. Use the library routine for a starting guess. A single iteration of Newton's method will then get very close to the double-precision answer, and two iterations will certainly do the trick.

5. One can compute $1/a$ by using Newton's method to find a zero of $f(x) = a-1/x$. The iteration is $x_{i+1} = 2x_i + ax_i^2$. Here is the convergence to the inverse of 0.9, starting at 1:

```
1.0000000000000000
1.1000000000000000
1.1110000000000000
1.1111111000000000
1.1111111111111110
1.1111111111111111
```

Do you see a pattern in the number of correct decimal digits at each step of the sequence?

6. Here is an Awk scaffolding program for studying Newton iteration. A typical input line to the program has three fields: a real number x whose root is to be computed, an initial value for the Newton iteration, and the number of iterations to perform.

```
function abs(x) { if (x < 0) x = -x; return x }
{   x = $1
    y = x
    rootx = sqrt(x)
    if (NF > 1)
        y = $2
    ub = 10
    if (NF > 2)
        ub = $3
    for (i = 1; i <= ub; i++) {
        printf "%5d: %25.16f %25.16f\n",
                i, y, abs(y-rootx)/rootx
        newy = .5*(y + x/y)
        if (newy == y) {
            print " Converged"
            break
        }
        y = newy
    }
}
```

If a number of iterations is not supplied, then the program provides a default value of ten. (It also stops when the sequence converges.) If a starting value is not supplied, then the program uses x itself.

8. J. L. Blue describes "A portable Fortran program to find the Euclidean norm of a vector" that avoids overflow and underflow in *ACM Transactions on Mathematical Software 4*, 1, March 1978, pp. 15–23.

9. See Solutions 11 and 12.

10. We can remove the first assignment by replacing Max with 2.0*Max:

```
Max := 0.5 * (2.0*Max + Sum/(2.0*Max))
```

and then algebraically manipulate it to

```
Max := Max + Sum/(4.0*Max)
```

to save one multiply and a few percent of the runtime of the routine.

11,12. Andrew Appel replaced K absolute values with a single one by keeping track of the largest square and then computing its absolute value outside the loop. (Bob Floyd observes that it might be cheaper to use a starting value based on the sum of the absolute values.) This code incorporates Appel's speedup and additionally uses table lookup for a good starting value. It is about ten percent faster than Program 4.

```
MaxT := T := A[1] - B[1]
MaxT2 := Sum := T*T
for J := 2 to K
    T := A[J] - B[J]
    T2 := T*T
    if T2 > MaxT2 then
        MaxT := T
        MaxT2 := T2
    Sum := Sum + T2
if Sum = 0.0 then return 0.0
if MaxT < 0.0 then MaxT := -MaxT
T := MaxT * DistTab[trunc(Scale*Sum/MaxT2)]
T :=   0.5 * (T + Sum/T)
return 0.5 * (T + Sum/T)
```

It uses a vector of floating point numbers initialized by

```
float DistTab[Scale..K*Scale]
for I := Scale to K*Scale do
    DistTab[I] = sqrt((I+0.5)/Scale)
```

I achieved single-precision accuracy with *Scale*=20. My original code for initializing the table used the system square root routine and took 0.3 seconds for K=16. I made it an order-of-magnitude faster by using the last square root computed as a starting guess and applying three Newton iterations.

14. W. Kahan's lecture notes on "Implementation of Algorithms" appeared as Berkeley Computer Science Technical Report #20 and are now available as National Technical Information Service Report AD-769 124. On page 52 of Section 19, Kahan shows that the routine in question may not terminate on an IBM 650; it can fail on other machines, as well.

15. Bob Floyd of Stanford University writes "If the ith approximation is off by a factor of f, the $i+1^{st}$ is off by a factor of $\phi(f) = (f+(1/f))/2$, where $\phi(f)=\phi(1/f)$, with smaller values between f and $1/f$, larger values outside. Clearly it is right to minimize the maximum abs log f."

Solutions for Column 15

1. Floyd and Rivest's paper in the March 1975 *Communications of the ACM* shows how sampling can be used to yield selection algorithms that are efficient in both theory and practice.

2. This loop-unrolled code sorts the array $X[1..3]$ in just three comparisons; the `assert` statements show the ordering established after each statement has been executed.

```
if X[1] > X[2] then
    swap(X[1], X[2])
assert X[1] < X[2]
if X[2] > X[3] then
    swap(X[2], X[3])
assert X[1] < X[3] and X[2] < X[3]
if X[1] > X[2] then
    swap(X[1], X[2])
assert X[1] < X[2] < X[3]
```

This is usually the fastest way to compute the median of three elements. To find the 1000th-smallest number on a tape of one million elements, one could read the tape while keeping the 1000 smallest numbers seen so far in a heap with the largest number on top.

3. A randomized binary search finds the median value of N numbers on a tape using a few variables and $O(\log N)$ passes over the tape. The variables L and U are lower and upper bounds of the range known to contain the median; they are initially the minimum and maximum elements in the set. Each stage of the algorithm makes two passes over the tape. The first pass stores in the variable M a random integer on the tape in the range $L..U$ (the first integer in the range is always stored in M, the second element in the range is stored with probability $1/2$, the third with probability $1/3$, and so forth). The second pass over the tape counts how many elements are less than M and how many elements are greater; M is then stored in either L or U. The process continues until M is the median value on the tape, which usually requires $O(\log N)$ passes over the tape, for an average total running time of $O(N \log N)$.

A second tape drive reduces the expected run time to $O(N)$ by keeping a tape that contains only elements currently in the range. Each pass over the tape consists of three phases. The first phase works as sketched above, the second phase copies active elements to the second tape, and a third phase copies them back to the first tape.

4. Blum, Floyd, Pratt, Rivest and Tarjan discovered a worst-case linear-time selection algorithm in the early 1970's. Most algorithms texts describe their algorithm in detail.

6. The variable C_N denotes the average value of *CCount* (N), the number of comparisons the selection algorithm uses to find the minimum element in an

N-element array. This program uses the recurrence relation for C_N given in the problem statement to print $C_0, C_1, ..., C_M$.

```
C[0] := C[1] := 0
print C[0], C[1]
for N := 2 to M do
    Sum := 0
    for I := 0 to N-1 do
        Sum := Sum + C[I]
    C[N] := N-1 + Sum/N
    print C[N]
```

Its $O(M^2)$ running time can be reduced to $O(M)$ by saving the previous value of *Sum*.

```
C[0] := C[1] := 0
print C[0], C[1]
Sum := C[0] + C[1]
for N := 2 to M do
    Sum := Sum + C[N-1]
    C[N] := N-1 + Sum/N
    print C[N]
```

The next code does away with the table $C[0..M]$ by storing $C[N]$ in the variable *LastC*.

```
Sum := 0
LastC := 0
print 0, 0
for N := 2 to M do
    Sum := Sum + LastC
    LastC := N-1 + Sum/N
    print LastC
```

One might use this program to examine the behavior of the algorithm experimentally. Alternatively, the structure of the program suggests a summation formula for C_N (converting the complicated recurrence into a summation is usually called "telescoping"). The solution is $C_N = 2(N-H_N)$, where H_N denotes the Nth harmonic number

$$1 + 1/2 + 1/3 + \cdots + 1/N$$

7. Algorithm 410 in the May 1971 *Communications of the ACM* "partially sorts" an array; it is due to John Chambers.

9. The first- and second-largest elements in a set can be found in $N + \log_2 N + O(1)$ comparisons. Knuth presents this and several other fascinating algorithms for computing order statistics using the optimal number of comparisons in Section 5.3.3 of his *Sorting and Searching*.

spots, popular night 73
square roots 4–7, 53, 72, 147–157, 189
stacks 23, 98
Starmer, C. F. vi, 40
State Machines, Finite 18–20, 24
Steele, G. L., Jr. 61–62, 66
stem-and-leaf graphs 118
Storer, D. 60
Stroustrup, B. vi, 101
structure diagrams, chemical 91–92
Strunk, W., Jr. 104–105, 112
subroutine libraries 33, 41, 84, 88–90,
    154, 167, 175–182, 198
supermarkets 75
surveys 47–49, 127–136, 195–196
symbol tables 23
syntax analysis 94–95
Szymanski, T. G. 8

tables 102–104
tables, symbol 23
tail recursion 31, 163
tapes 201
Tarjan, R. E. 201
Tbl 102
testing 8, 23, 27–36, 54, 57, 59–60, 77,
    155, 187
tests, quick 4, 32, 75
TEX 101, 109
THESEUS-II 77–79
Thompson, K. L. 58, 119
time-series graphs 119
topological sorting 20–23
tradeoffs 33, 50, 78–79, 101, 197–198
trails, audit 41
transmission, data 47–48, 52
trees, binary search 24, 185, 197
Trickey, H. W. vi, 11
Troff 101
Tufte, E. R. 122, 124, 126, 135
Tukey, J. W. 118, 195–196
Tukey, P. A. 123, 194
typesetting figures 105–107

ugly graphs 122, 136
Ullman, J. D. 99

Vyssotsky, V. A. vi, 59, 67, 77, 79

Washington, G. 118
Weide, B. W. vi, 73, 75, 191

weighted medians 169–170
Weinberger, P. J. 10, 25, 59, 172
Weir, W. 60
West Point 48
White, E. B. 104–105, 112
white space 108
Whiteside, B. 66
Whorf, B. 15, 112
Whorf's hypothesis 15, 112
Williams, H. H. 65
Williamson, H. 113
wine cellars 73
Wintz, P. 11
Woodard, G. 189
word counts 9, 17, 115–118
Wulf, W. A. 18, 67

Yacc 94–98

Zerouni, C. 59, 64